W9-CCX-578

LACEY FOSBURGH

WITHDRAWN

TIME

THE
TRUE STORY
OF THE
"GOODBAR"
MURDER

DELACORTE PRESS/NEW YORK

098039

Red Wing Public Library
Red Wing, MN 55066

Published by
Delacorte Press
1 Dag Hammarskjold Plaza
New York, New York 10017

Some of the material in this work is based upon articles by the author that
first appeared in *New Times* and *Cosmopolitan*.

Copyright © 1975, 1977 by Lacey Fosburgh

All rights reserved. No part of this book may be reproduced in any form or
by any means without the prior written permission of the Publisher,
excepting brief quotes used in connection with reviews written specifically
for inclusion in a magazine or newspaper.
Manufactured in the United States of America
Second Printing—1977
Designed by MaryJane DiMassi

Library of Congress in Publication Data
Fosburgh, Lacey, 1942–
    Closing time.

    1. Murder—New york (City)—Case studies.
2. Cleary, Katherine, 1944–1973.   3. Simpson, Joe
Willie, 1949–1973.   I. Title
HV6534.N5F67   364.1'523'0926   77–14548

ISBN 0-440-01371-2

(4)

RED WING PUBLIC LIBRARY
0 1040 00303303

BWB

.25

364.1523 Fosburgh, Lacey,
C58f   χ   1942-

          Closing time
098039

DATE			

Red Wing Public Library
Red Wing, MN 55066

© THE BAKER & TAYLOR CO.

CLOSING TIME

CLOSING

To ARTHUR GELB and WALLY TURNER,

for years of support and respect
and their own shining examples there ahead of me.

With much love.

PROLOGUE

I DON'T REMEMBER how I first heard about this murder, but it must have been when Arthur Gelb, then the Metropolitan Editor at the *New York Times,* called my name and assigned me to cover it. All I know is the murder had just happened and that at that time there was only one side to it: Her name was Katherine Cleary and she was the one who was dead.

It was January in New York City and there had been a lot of murders that winter. This was yet another. But while most of the others were ignored by the media, this was not. There was no very good reason why the case of Katherine Cleary was singled out, except the victim was a classic archetype: She was a young schoolteacher, pretty, Irish Catholic, and decent—just the kind of person who should not end up the way she did—and for some reason the media, in its collective sense of outcry, covered her death.

There was another reason the case aroused public interest. It was a mystery. The killer had escaped, and until he was identified and found, the story remained on the front pages. Then, predictably, as soon as the killer was arrested, the media lost interest, and the case of Katherine Cleary vanished as quickly as it had arrived.

But although the case disappeared from the newspapers, the murder itself, from the very beginning, had been the kind of emblematic crime people always remember. It was a story of death and violence, a tale of innocence plucked and life arbitrarily closed, a victim and the slayer, the innocent and the foul. People saw in it the specter of random violence haunting the city streets. The killer was safe, the schoolteacher, the personification of innocence, was dead. It was a mythic tale and it disturbed people who saw in her going an arbitrariness that frightened them, violence unleashed without reason.

At first it was the death of this quiet, compelling woman —and the mystery of her death—that started my fascination with this story. But then, afterward, when public interest in the case was over, and I saw the man who killed her, with his head bent over toward the left and his eyes peering round the sides, I became curious about him, too. I wanted to know why it had happened.

They had known each other less than two or three hours, so why? What had happened? What went wrong?

This has led, three years later, to a book about the lives of these two people. As far as I can tell, everything happened the way I've written it. I was there at the beginning as a reporter for the *New York Times* in New York, walking 72nd Street, talking to police, going to the morgue.

I have researched this material on and off for three years, first, of course, for the *Times* and then for a magazine piece and finally for a book. I have traveled to Illinois, New Jersey, New York, and Miami, and since during the intervening years I have moved to San Francisco, I have crossed the country four times in search of more information.

I have talked to virtually everyone mentioned in the story. The family of Joe Willie Simpson cooperated thoroughly. They took me into their house and gave me milk and toast and brought out photographs and letters and talked for hours. They even went back through all the areas of pain and talked about hospitals and money, a rabbit and a cat. I respect them tremendously for this. According to my way of thinking, they honored themselves and their son by telling me what they knew.

Carole Musty, too, on a hot winter night in north Miami, curled up on a couch with a Tab and said as much as she could remember. Steve Levine helped, too, when he leaned back in the shadows of the wooden room where it all started and brought out his memories. He said it made him wish he could travel in the desert.

At first Danny Murray refused to see me. Then he agreed to meet in a public cafeteria, and there he sat in silence and drank coffee and played with his spoon. Ever so slowly he began to talk, and since then, for the last three years, he has shared as much with me as I think he could and my respect and affection for him are boundless. He realized, I think, that a book about Joe Willie and Katherine would, ironically, give Joe Willie some of the dignity and recognition he had not had elsewhere.

There is one major exception in all this. Vincent and

Mary Cleary, Katherine's parents, refused to see me. I talked to them several times on the telephone, not long, but enough to get a sense of their warmth and kindness. I understand their unwillingness to talk, but I regret it: I know there is more to Katherine Cleary than I was able to discover.

I did catch a glimpse of her, but unfortunately many of the people who really knew her chose not to share that knowledge with me. I wish I could do her more justice in the story that follows because I think she deserved it and because I, as a woman, think her drama was one that many women, myself included, have lived. She and the rest of us are pioneers, of sorts, developing our own role models as we go along, with only our own track records to guide us. It's hard, but the fascination of Katherine, of course, is that this was what she was dealing with. She could have done better, but for my part, I wish I knew more about the options and choices she faced.

Out of all this research and time and travel I have written what I call an interpretive biography. To the best of my knowledge everything here is true. After much thought, though, I have changed the names in the story and altered several identifying features. In some cases, I did this upon request and in others, at my own initiative, because I figured the amount of pain this drama caused everyone was sufficient; let the people have as much privacy as they can.

I have described the wind and the fields; I have re-created scenes and written dialogue and said what people thought and felt, and all this is based on factual accounts of what occurred. In addition, a few times I have stepped in where full and accurate accounts do not exist and created scenes or dialogue I think it reasonable and fair to assume could have taken place, perhaps even did.

What I have done, then, is give myself the liberty to go beyond proven fact to probe the internal and private lives of the people involved in this story. That is why I call it an interpretive biography.

For me this format was essential in order to make Joe Willie and Katherine come alive and tell us, as I think they can, about the violence and loneliness, repression and sadness in all of us. These two people were just trying their best to get to tomorrow, and they didn't always have a lot of luck.

But I don't consider either one of them strange or bizarre. They are, instead, much like the rest of us, and the significance of Katherine Cleary and Joe Willie Simpson is not, therefore, that they are different, or unique, but, rather, that they are familiar.

CLOSING TIME

As a remedy to life in society, I would suggest living in the big city. Nowadays it is the only desert within our means.

ALBERT CAMUS

1

THE ONE-ROOM APARTMENT where she lived was
full of silence and solitude. Every now and then a car
passed in the street outside or there was the sound of
ships in the harbor or garbage cans blowing along the
sidewalk. Otherwise, it was still and lonely and cold.

She lay in bed all morning. She was Katherine Cleary,
and not very many people knew her name or recognized
her face. It was Monday, January first, and she was twenty-
eight years old. She was not going to get any older. She
was not going to wake up tomorrow morning, and all the
privacy and solitariness of her life was slipping away fast.

New York was a cold wintry gray. Harry Truman had
just died and the seven Watergate burglars were about to
go on trial. It was 1973. There were somewhere between
six and seven million people living in New York that day,

and what may have been the first murder of the year was about to happen.

It was not yet moments away, but the last hours had begun, and two people who had never met were getting closer and closer. Yesterday they had been thousands of miles apart. Today, they were separated by just three blocks. They had no rendezvous, no common friends, no reason to meet, but in just a few hours they would come together, and just a few hours after that, one would die and the other would disappear.

The night before was New Year's Eve, and Katherine Cleary had spent the hours alone in an apartment fifteen feet wide and twenty feet long. The telephone didn't ring and the doorbell didn't sound. She heard no "Auld Lang Syne" or party whistles, no champagne fizzing or glasses touching. It had just been very quiet.

And now on the holiday morning it was still quiet. Her only companion was a cat who licked her own insides, a cat she watched in fascination and envy, and with even a touch of hate. The cat was luscious and aloof, a female infatuated with her own beauty, and Katherine Cleary, after all, was not.

Her room was a mess, a tumult of clothes and books, dirty plates and rotting food. Underpants and torn stockings, jeans and sweaters and bras were lying everywhere. The dishes stacked in the sink dated back to Saturday night, the thirtieth, when a man called Richard had come. The black frying pan was still caked with leftover scrambled eggs; and yesterday, Sunday, she had waited all day hoping another man would call. He never did. She had started to read *Deliverance,* and had eaten sandwiches and spaghetti.

The book was about the land deep in the southern wilderness where a wild river ran. And on the last full night of her life, Katherine Cleary was carried along, as if by the river itself, by the tale of violence and rape and murder, death and male dreams.

Afterward, when it was all over, the detective named Cooley would look down at her bedside table and tell the men named Kraft and McBride, "Hey, look what she was reading." And he would notice that she might have finished the book if she had not decided to go out instead.

But sometime Monday, January first, Katherine Cleary did get up out of bed and put on her clothes. Three blocks to the south, in his best friend's apartment high on a thirty-second floor, Joe Willie Simpson, in his blue plaid undershorts, awoke about four in the afternoon and got dressed. He talked to Danny and he played with the iguana named Rover. Then sometime later he and Danny went out for dinner.

At about the same time, Katherine decided that she would not stay at home alone, as she had the night before. She would go out across the street, as she often did, to her own special place of connections—a small neighborhood bar called Tweed's.

THE CITY WAS COLD that night and there was no moon. The berths along the Hudson were plated with ice, and wind careened down the streets and passed the corners. The sky was clouded, without stars. It was the kind of night when no one should be outside or alone.

O'Jack, the newsdealer on the corner of West 72nd Street and Broadway, remembered a large dog scruffing up and down, "Looking for a doorway." It came by every night, he said, a hound that had no home. Monday it shuffled down the street, hanging in close to the buildings as if to miss as much of the wind as possible. The *Times* delivery truck came by once, too, O'Jack said, but that was all, except for the dog.

Over there, on Manhattan's West Side, the streets were almost empty, and even 72nd Street, with its all-night delicatessens and places where egg rolls and soup cost less than a dollar, was deserted. It was too cold.

No one stood on the corner reading the early editions or eating hot dogs. There were none of the usual junkies who leaned against the lamp posts like forgotten canes; and there was no one in Needle Park, where, for a decade or more, people found their versions of life in packets of white powder and a shivery sensation in the spine.

It was the beginning of a new year, but the celebration

was over. This was January first and it was cold and quiet
and the only sound was an occasional taxicab or the subway underneath.

O'Jack remembered the quiet because, blind in eyes, he
dealt in the land of noise, and that night, he said, there was
none except for the wind. The only action at his place was
Long John's all-night talk show and the dog, licking at his
glove, and then the sound of him pushing up against the
metal doorways as he went off down the block toward
West End Avenue.

Farther down in that direction, where the residential
buildings began and the commercial places ended, was
Tweed's Bar. It stood on the south side of 72nd Street
near the corner of West End Avenue, and all that was
visible of it from the street was the pair of steps heading
down.

Once there had been a window there, but long ago
wooden planks were barricaded over the spot to keep out
the cold and the thieves, and just now these planks shook
in the wind like an old barn door.

Inside, the wind was leaking through the cracks in the
wood and hissing like steam in a radiator. The street was
cold but Tweed's was hot and crowded. A mist of smoke
hung in the air like urban smog and people, back to back,
hip to hip, filled the small channel by the door between
the bar and the jukebox. In the back the tables in the long
narrow room were full, and by midnight the air was almost
rancid. It smelled of liquor and smoke, hamburgers and
sweat, and, every now and then, the scent of weed wafted
through the crowd like a conversation faintly overheard.

Joe Willie Simpson was there, drinking alone at the bar.

Danny had gone home. He said he wanted to start the New Year right. Joe Willie liked the sound of the noise and the feel of the glass. He sat on the stool at the far end, close to the cash register, and listened to the music and the voices in the room and the words inside his head.

His hair was blond, his eyes blue, his face strong and bony.

Afterward no one remembered him.

Katherine Cleary was there, too, drinking alone at the opposite end of the bar. Her long red hair covered much of her face, and her eyes were serious. She may have wished, as she often did, that everything could be different for her, and that she had something like a white lace gown or a penthouse in the sky where people came to dinner.

She sat in the dim shadows of the bar. The pretty profile of her pale face stood out against the dark walls behind her, and she must have looked a bit like a child. In a while, she would move out into the crowd. She didn't want to be alone. But now she was just holding her glass and listening to the noise. Somebody was talking about the day's football game; on the jukebox Leonard Cohen was singing about "Suzanne, our lady of the flowers," and Katherine might have thought of Easter lilies.

Around her the wooden walls were aging and cracked, and spider plants hung from the ceiling, their green and white trails dangling in the air. There were photographs everywhere, shades of sepia and brown, of a past New York and forgotten people, and they hung somehow permanently crooked, as if they had adjusted through the years to the shiftings of the earth. The place had no air of happiness or peace of mind. It was like a backwater eddy where time and the water were caught, where lost dreams and worry swirled on the smoke.

West 72nd Street isn't Park Avenue and Tweed's wasn't ever the Ritz. There were no linens or expense accounts. Over here at Tweed's there were no bouncers, no check-room, no uniforms. Nobody ordered Brandy Alexanders and there weren't even any towels in the bathroom. Tweed's had everything the street could offer—there was hustle and tension and high-pitched laughter. Drugs were shared in the bathroom. The hamburger smelled of grease. Drinks were cheap, sex was often cheaper, and no one ever had to go home at night alone.

And so it happened that Katherine Cleary did not go home alone that Monday night. Joe Willie Simpson went with her, and when he left a little while later, the savagery was over, and Katherine Cleary lay twisted on her back on the sheets of the bed. A box of granulated sugar was spilled at her feet and traces of her life were splattered in red all over the wall.

Joe Willie Simpson, a stranger who said he was Charlie Smith, took the elevator back down to the street and dis-appeared. But before he left, he took a white nylon slip framed with lace from a bureau drawer. He rubbed it along the tables and the doorknobs, the clock by the win-dow, and the can on the shelf where the grass was kept.

Still naked, he stepped into the shower and washed the blood off his body. He would forget to turn off the faucet, and the slow stream of water would run cold and unno-ticed for two days. After the shower, Joe Willie put on his shirt and pants and the brown leather jacket he liked so much, and left. He carried the white nylon slip in his hand,

and in the elevator he rubbed it along the knobs and the walls. Later the next day, safe in another place, he threw it down an incinerator chute.

The wind blew through the night, and in the morning the sky was overcast. It was Tuesday, January second; the Christmas holidays were over. Buses and subways were crowded with schoolchildren, and up north in the Bronx, at St. Joseph's School for the Deaf, twenty-eight-year-old Katherine Cleary did not show up for work.

The Catholic sisters assigned a substitute teacher to take her place in the classroom and someone called her home. There was no answer.

At lunch break a friend looked for her as usual in the cafeteria. She was not there, and one of the children said, "Katherine is sick." The friend called her at home, but there was no answer.

Later that night, over in Tweed's, the owner, a man named Steve Levine, thought about her and wondered if she'd come by, but she didn't.

The next day, Wednesday, Katherine didn't come to school, and she didn't answer the phone. Suddenly her absence seemed odd, and the principal sent a teacher down to knock on her door on West 72nd Street.

Now he stood there in the hallway and tried the door. There was no answer. He heard Missy, the cat, inside, meowing. The hallway was dim. One of the lightbulbs had burned out. He stood by the elevator waiting for it to come and then, instead of going back to school, he went to find the superintendent.

"Have you seen Katherine Cleary lately?" he asked the man.

"No, not in a while."

"I'm from the school where she works and she hasn't shown up for two days," he said. "Her phone doesn't answer, and they think something could have happened to her."

"I don't know."

"The cat's there. Can you let me into her place to see?"

It was 9:25. They went back up to the seventh floor and the super tried first one key, then the other. They didn't fit. "Sorry," he said.

The third key slipped into place and turned, and as the door opened, Missy, the cat, ran screeching past their legs out into the hall.

AT POLICE HEADQUARTERS an emergency call for help was received about a minute later and transmitted electronically to all squad cars in the area and the 20th Precinct on West 82nd Street.

There Detective Tom Cooley took the call. A murder in 253 West 72nd, Apartment 715; victim, a white female.

This was the beginning. He had a pad of paper in his pocket, a .38-caliber pistol at his waist, and with four other detectives—including his partner Louie McBride, and Lt. Michael Kraft—he went south to 72nd Street.

This was the heart of the Upper West Side of Manhattan, an area with one of the highest crime rates in the city and a population made up of all colors and inclinations. There were people here rich enough to have limousines with stereos and refrigerators, while others lived on dog food, starch and welfare payments. The very rich and the very poor lived side by side. People talked about political reform and civil liberties, women worked for day care and equality, and everybody worried about education, yet, tucked in all the corners were other people who were forgotten, overlooked, and depressed.

This was the West Side, and here the fear of crime and violence was as real as the garbage and the dirt. Like a virus, the fear attacked everybody—the old and the lonely, the families with homes and bicycles, and the people like Katherine who were young and single and working.

There had already been one murder down the street and another two blocks north. There had been slayings in an old hotel several streets to the east, and recently a woman had been slashed to death by an assailant who sped off into the night with her pocketbook. The week before, on Christmas Eve, a man was stabbed waiting for a bus up the street on Broadway, and two nights earlier, a block away in another direction, a payroll messenger was shot. He, too, had died.

In the past other young women, some of them school-teachers, had been murdered in the area, but, still, Katherine's death was not only the latest. It would be the worst.

Cooley, McBride and Kraft reached 72nd Street and parked outside Two-Five-Three. There they saw the dull gray lobby for the first time, the small shiny elevators with the black buttons, and the hallway upstairs where the murderer had fled.

Inside, they saw what the murderer had left behind.

The small, boxlike room was totally disarranged, as if someone had overturned everything in sight, and right in the center, spread out in the middle of the double bed, was the body of a young woman. She was covered from the throat to the knees with a turquoise-blue silk bathrobe. It appeared to have been thrown over her afterward. Her long thick red hair was sprayed out behind her head like a crown.

Her skin was the awful color of white that meant she was dead, and along the edges of the bathrobe, her neck was covered with a brown chalky substance Cooley knew was blood that had dried for days and then cracked.

Above her head, spread out on the wall like a gigantic mural, was a wild, ragged spray of red. It, too, was blood, and there, where it seeped into the paint, it made an ominous, bewildering picture.

The men stopped in the doorway, stunned.

The woman was lying on her back with her left leg stuck straight out over the end of the bed. Her right leg, spread at a wide angle to the left, was bent at the knee. Her arms were bent at the elbows, and her little hands were at shoulder level with their palms up. They looked as if they had fallen there, exhausted, defeated, after trying to push something away. The bathrobe concealed her nude torso and whatever had been done there was out of sight.

The woman's face was small and delicate, with bruises on both the right and the left cheeks and the forehead. The nose and the lips were severely swollen and purple.

Right up next to her face was a thirty-six-inch-long white cement statue. It was a carving of a woman's face and looked, in fact, like the victim. The two identical faces, one cold flesh, the other cold stone, stared directly at each other, nose to nose.

It was a strange, disjointed scene. The woman's eyes were not open in horror or shock, as eyes usually are in violent death. They were closed, as if she were asleep. And the woman herself looked lovely, young. Strangely, even with the bruises and the sureness of blood and mess beneath the robe, she seemed graceful and serene.

"Good fucking Christ," Lieutenant Kraft said quietly.

The men began making their way carefully into the room, sidestepping clothes, books, and overturned chairs.

"Hey, look what she was reading," said Cooley, pointing to the book open beside her bed.

"Well," said Kraft giving orders, "we can't touch anything until the lab boys get here." He checked his watch. "Five, ten minutes. That means we don't touch the robe or look at the body, but," he said, gazing around the little room, "let's go over it quick, see what we can find. A weapon, maybe."

He shook his head. He seemed sad, personally affronted by the violence.

Cooley went into the bathroom, on the left of the entrance foyer. The water in the shower was running and he looked around the curtains and behind the door, but found nothing. He left the water on so the handles could be checked for prints.

Outside, on the right side of the tiny foyer, was the makeshift kitchen. Kraft, McBride, and the others—Detectives Flynt and Clines—searched the room, looking for something, anything, that would give them information about the murder or the murderer. Cooley studied the sink, filthy and covered with dirty dishes and pans. There was a knife on the counter. It was a five-inch-long carving knife with a bone handle, but the steel blade had been bent in the middle, almost at a right angle, as if it had pushed against something very, very hard.

"Kraft," he said. "Look at this."

McBride and the lieutenant came across the room and peered down at the shiny metal knife.

"Looks like it's been cleaned off," said McBride.

Kraft agreed. "But let the lab boys have it," he said.

They didn't find anything else. But they looked. The room had one window, about four feet square, a radiator, a rhododendron plant, a Snoopy dog and a Snoopy Christmas card, and several thick fat red candles standing on the windowsill. There were also armchairs, bureaus, books, and, on one table, two eight-by-eleven-inch drawings. Lying on a pile of magazines, the drawings had once, clearly, been rolled tight, but now they were loose and unraveled. Cooley looked at them. They were unsigned. One was a picture of Donald Duck, the other of Mickey Mouse.

About ten minutes later the others arrived, the lab technicians, photographers, and people from the medical examiner's office. They brought plastic bags, trays, cameras, tweezers, ointments, magnifying glasses, cans of black fingerprint dusting powder, and rubber gloves.

"We got a knife over here in the sink," Kraft said. "It may be the weapon. But the bed's your first move."

"The blood on her neck is old," the man from the medical examiner's staff said. "I can tell from here."

Kraft nodded. "I know."

The technicians moved around the bed and looked for pieces of hair or cloth or anything else in the folds of the bathrobe. They also took dozens of color photographs that would later look garish and bright in the manila files. Then they lifted the white statue off the bed and put it in a green plastic box. Afterward they took different corners of the blue bathrobe and carefully lifted it off the body as if it were a tablecloth covered with crumbs.

Underneath, fully exposed, was Katherine Cleary.

Nobody said anything. They just looked at the body. It was a mess.

She was naked and splotched from the neck to the crotch with patches of dark, dry blood. Her skin was torn and ripped in what turned out to be eighteen places in the neck and the stomach. Her twisted body looked like a doll that had been dropped and broken. The wounds, however, had already begun to disappear, the way they do in death when two sides of a cut close in on the middle and look like lips tightening over gums with no teeth. The blood that had gushed from the wounds had dried and cracked and she looked now on Wednesday morning as if she had been buried for years in hard brown mud.

Six of the stab wounds were in the neck and the other twelve in the stomach. One dug as far down in the belly as the abdominal cavity; another reached the liver. The enormous jugular vein in the neck was completely severed and the body was covered with bruises, on her neck, arms, wrists, and around her thighs.

Ironically, the worst and final discovery was also the least. It probably hadn't killed her and it might not even have hurt. Her thighs were spread wide, far beyond the normal angle, and she looked as if she had been cracked in half there at the center.

And there, in her most private, intimate place, her vagina was thrust up in the air. It was no longer shrouded in modesty and protected beneath the muff of pubic hair, brown and curly. Instead it was gaping up, like a mouth, wide and open, raw and red and high.

And plunged down into it, like a giant penis, was a thick fat red candle.

It seemed at least halfway out of sight.

4

JOE WILLIE SIMPSON was asleep in the Sunnyside Hotel in downtown Miami. He arrived late Tuesday and registered as Jack Samuels.

There was a twenty-nine-cent packet of aspirins open on the table by the bed and a small prescription bottle less than half full of yellow capsules. The label, from a New York pharmacy, read: "Daniel P. Murray. Take one before sleeping."

The room cost $9.50 and overlooked the back end of a drugstore and a porno theater. The curtains were rust-colored with gilt fringe, the rug a dirty gray, and the only other furniture was a television set, which was turned on, and a chest of drawers. A New York/Miami plane ticket lay crumpled on the floor.

The man was lying on his back, his mouth slightly open. He had thrown off the covers and was naked except for his blue plaid undershorts.

A pillow was propped up behind his head and there were thin scratch marks all over his chest. They were still bright red with dry blood and they stretched all the way from his throat down to his belly button.

When he first arrived in Miami, sometime Tuesday, he flopped down on the bed and stared at the television set. He was exhausted; every part of his body ached. He thought he was getting a cold.

His back, his shoulders, and his arms hurt the most. His head, too, was in a continuous kind of circulating pain and he wished Carole was there to give him a massage. He tried pressing his fingers against the temples or between his eyes, but it did no good.

It was, he told himself, a cold. He hadn't been getting enough sleep.

He didn't move for hours. His mind was blank. Every now and then he wondered about what he should do. But he didn't think about what he had done.

THE VICTIM'S NAME was Katherine Cleary, the super told Cooley, Katherine C-l-e-a-r-y. She was a nice girl. She was quiet and well-behaved and she always paid her rent on time.

The woman was a teacher, the man from St. Joseph's School said. She specialized in teaching the deaf and she knew how to read lips and make sign language. Her folks lived in New Jersey, in a place called Holyoke, and they were Catholic, he said. It was a good middle-class family. She was a good girl, he went on, a good person and she had lots of friends.

Cooley was talking to them in the hallway. He was taking notes. The rest of the detectives and the lab boys were still at work in the apartment.

Katherine Cleary wasn't the kind of person who had enemies, the schoolteacher and the super agreed, and, no, they didn't think she had a steady boyfriend. They had no idea who could have done it. This is a bad neighborhood, they added. It could have been an addict or a burglar.

Cooley took down their names and telephone numbers. He didn't have to remind them this was serious, he said, and if they had any ideas he'd appreciate it if they got in touch right away.

The work had begun. The investigation was under way. They had her address book and her pile of letters. They had snapshots and notebooks. They knew where she worked and where she came from, but now they had the hardest part left to do. They had to find her life and discover her habits. They had to locate her friends, her acquaintances, and ascertain when or where a stranger could fit in. They had to turn her life into a file of records, information, dates, times, places, and people so that in the end there would be no blank places, no mysteries, no unknowns, and no privacy.

Sometime around noon the homicide detectives went back down the little elevator to the street. Upstairs the lab

technicians were still at work in the apartment; one man
with a can of black fingerprint powder had turned to Kraft
and said, "Hey, Lieutenant."

"Yeah?"

"Hate to tell you this, but doesn't look like there're any
prints here."

"What do you mean?"

"Place looks like it's been wiped clean."

Kraft shook his head.

"Tell you another thing," the man went on.

"What?"

"There's nothing here."

"What do you mean?"

"I mean we still got a lot of checking to do, but the way
things look now, I don't think we got anything. No clues
or leads. I don't think we got anything."

The detectives left and after a while the photographers
would leave too, then the men with the plastic boxes and
the equipment, and finally the long metal stretcher covered with the sheet would be wheeled out and Katherine
Cleary would be on her way to the morgue.

Downstairs the sun was beginning to shine through the
clouds, and 72nd Street was very much alive. It was no
longer a holiday, and the place was full of cars and noise
and people. The men stood and talked for a while and
then Clines and Flynt went one way, Kraft another, and
Tom Cooley and Louie McBride another.

Kraft had told them to check the immediate vicinity of
72nd Street to see if anyone knew the deceased. Stores,
bars, he said, and later they'd all meet back upstairs in the
apartment.

Not many people down here on the street had heard about the murder of Katherine Cleary yet and they weren't going to read about it in the newspapers for two days, not until Friday.

A clerk in the 20th Precinct on West 82nd Street neglected Wednesday to list the murder among the so-called unusuals he sent down to police headquarters every morning. He sent word about a suicide two blocks away and he mentioned some robberies, but the name of Katherine Cleary was not in the "Unusual Crime Report," and so, later that day, down at headquarters, reporters thumbing through these sheets saw nothing about the school-teacher.

The first person Cooley and McBride told about the murder was the proprietor of a store next door to the building at Two-Five-Three. He was a small dark-haired man and, sure, he said, he remembered Katherine Cleary. "We get some weird people around here," he told them, "but this girl was different. She was very nice and quiet and shy."

Their next stop was a bar on the other side of the building. It was called the Copper Hatch and it had a glass-enclosed deck that extended out into the sidewalk, tables with candles and red linen, and a long clean counter inside.

Of course, the people there said, we know Katherine Cleary. She's a regular. Comes in two, three, four, nights a week. Why? No kidding. Terrible. She was a good kid. Hung out here, the bartender said. This is a nice place, he added, not a singles bar, just a friendly neighborhood place.

Cooley's eyes got accustomed to the dark and he and McBride talked to the staff, took the names of several people who were her friends. He was trying to get a sense of the woman who, paradoxically, only meant something to him in her death. The way he worked, he looked first for some kind of basic picture of the victim's character— or the murderer's—and then as rapidly as possible tried to flesh out that image with more reality, nuance, and substance.

So far all he had was a blank. A nice young attractive schoolteacher who, like himself, was Catholic.

"When'd you see her last?" he asked the bartender.

"Hard to tell. People come in and outta here all the time. Get a Coke. Get a beer. Cash a check. Hey, you seen so and so? Hard to remember exactly when." But he said it seemed to him she'd been there Monday, January first.

"Was she alone?"

"That's hard to tell," he said. "She knew everyone and so I mighta seen her talking to someone but not know if she was actually with him."

"What was she doing?" Cooley asked.

"Talking. She was one of these people, Officer, had two moods. She could be loud, and I mean loud; or quiet, almost withdrawn."

Cooley and McBride listened.

"Seems to me like she was talking. At the bar. I think some of her girlfriends were here. On Monday, a group of them came over late from Tweed's."

"She was part of that group?" McBride asked.

"I think so," said the man, and then he added, "You know, she was crippled or something, don't ya?"

"Crippled? What do you mean?"

"I don't know. She limped. Accident or something."

After a while Cooley and McBride finished asking questions and went back out into the sunshine. They looked at each other. They were both tall and large and red-headed. They were also Irish Catholic, and they loved the intensity and unpredictability of their work.

They were smart, too. They knew how to look and listen, and they were known throughout the police department as master professionals.

"Tweed's?" said McBride.

Cooley nodded.

They crossed the street and went inside. Tweed's was empty except for a man with dark hair sitting at the counter. He had a notebook and a pile of receipts in front of him.

As they walked in, he looked at them.

They came down the room and introduced themselves. "We're investigating a murder," Cooley said. "Across the street. Girl by the name of Katherine Cleary. You know her?"

The man didn't answer. It was cold in there. The heat hadn't come on yet and he was still wearing his windbreaker. There were dirty glasses from the night before still on the bar and the sounds from the street sounded muted, far away.

"You know her?" McBride asked.

The man nodded. "What happened to her?"

"We found her this morning in her apartment. Murdered."

The man didn't say anything.

"D'you know her for long?" McBride asked.

"What?" the man asked.

"You know her for long?"

"Seven, eight years. I was very close to her," he said quietly.

The room was still. Cooley looked at the man closely. He had dark eyes, strong hands, and a good face. He was about thirty years old. "What's your name?" he asked him, as he reached in his pocket for the notebook.

"Steve Levine."

"You work here?"

"No. I'm the owner. What happened to her?"

"She got pretty cut up. Looks like she coulda been raped first."

"When?"

"Don't know. Probably at least a day or two ago."

"Any idea who did it?" Steve asked.

"That's what we'd like to talk to you about."

"Jesus Christ," the man said, putting his head in his hands. "I don't know. Goddamn Katherine . . . she was such a hardworking little thing. I'll have to think about it. I can probably help you a lot. I want to help as much as I can, but I haven't seen her in a couple of days. Not since Monday night."

"You sure?"

"Yes. She didn't come in last night."

"Is that unusual?"

"Not necessarily. She came in all the time. She was one of the regulars, but, still, a couple of days could go by and she wouldn't come in. Usually, though, she'd stop by. But she was moody."

"Badly?" asked Cooley. He was trying to get a sense of the woman.

"Yes, sometimes. She was in here for several hours Monday night," Steve went on. "Came in around nine or ten. Left about one. I think she went across the street to the Copper Hatch. A group of them did."

"Did she have a date? Or was she with someone?"

"I don't think so. Katherine was the kind of person knew lots of people and if she was in a certain mood she'd be talking up a storm with everybody in sight. I think Monday was one of those nights."

"Can you give us some names?"

Steve mentioned several and then said, "There's one guy you should find. He wasn't here that night, but he didn't like Katherine. Freddie Watson. He beat her up once."

Cooley wrote the name down. "Freddie Watson." He put two large asterisks by his name.

"But Monday," Steve continued, "she talked to a lot of folks. It was pretty much the regular crowd."

"We'll have to check them all out," McBride said.

Steve nodded. "And there was one guy I never saw before."

"What'd he look like?"

"I don't know. I don't remember him at all. I just remember Katherine with someone, right here, by the cash register."

"Were they together? Friends? A pickup?"

. "No," said Steve. "I don't think so. Just talking. But I'll tell you who might know more. The night bartender, Jack Pawling."

6

ON WEDNESDAY, THE same day, Danny Murray, Joe Willie Simpson's best friend, went to work, but once there he told his secretary he was sick and he went back home. He had called on Tuesday, too, to say he wasn't coming in. The flu, he supposed, and she said, laughing, was he sure it wasn't just New Year's? He was the executive in charge of finances for a large advertising company and he didn't have the flu.

He was worried about Joe Willie. Joe Willie had told him about the murder.

Now it was January third. He lifted the iguana named Rover out of the bathtub and took a shower. Afterward he sat in the living room in his bathrobe. The curtains were still pulled, and his view of the Hudson River and the New Jersey hills was obscured. Nothing had changed since Monday night, when Joe Willie told him what happened.

The place was enclosed, dark. There were ships out there and palisades and sky as far as the eye could see, but Danny Murray just stared at the heavy blue material hanging over the window.

He'd never felt more disturbed in his life. His hands were sweating. His outstretched palms were enormous, and, looking at them now, he could actually see his hands shake. He was smoking, lighting each cigarette from the end of the last. And he sat there on the couch, rubbing his hands along his knees to keep them dry.

He didn't know what to think. There was nothing in the newspapers. He'd looked, and now he was totally bewildered. He wondered if Joe Willie could possibly have been lying about the murder.

He thought for a long while and then he got up and went to the kitchen. He bent down on his knees in front of the sink and began to search through the cabinet. There were the soaps and polish Carole had bought, the box of iguana food and plenty of other things, but he couldn't find the black plastic gloves.

Later he found them in the closet in the bathroom. He put them in his pocket and went outside. It was almost four o'clock.

AT JUST ABOUT THAT time, Tom Cooley and Louie McBride headed back toward the apartment.

They had ventured into Katherine's world, and in her death she was coming alive to them. She told jokes, she talked too much, and she got too loud, or else, too quiet, and she always carried a book. They were beginning to get a hint of contradiction, a sense of her highs and lows.

They had been up and down the block, on both sides of the street, and as far as they could figure out she had been only to Tweed's and the Copper Hatch that night. They were putting together a couple of lists: one of everyone who'd seen her Monday, a second of friends, acquaintances. Everyone would have to be questioned.

Cooley and McBride got most of their information in the bars. They'd been to the nice ones with napkins and olives, the in-between places like Tweed's and the Hatch, and then real down-and-out dives like the Green Oaks Bar several blocks away on Broadway. Katherine Cleary was even a regular there, too, it turned out. The place seemed to specialize in pimps, hookers, addicts, and bikers, and the two cops acknowledged in a silent way that that jarred their impression of the nice little schoolteacher.

But even there no one said anything bad about her. She drank, but she didn't drink too much. She got loud, even raucous, but she never got ugly or indecent, and she knew a lot of people, a lot of men, but there was never any suggestion she slept around. She was "nice, well-behaved," the bartender said.

Back at the building the super was waiting in the lobby. "Find anything?" he asked.

They shook their heads.

McBride and Cooley took the elevator to the seventh floor. The apartment door was open. Kraft, Flynt, and Clines were already there, sitting around the room, looking serious.

Kraft was on the windowsill. "The lock wasn't jimmied," he told the detectives.

"Sure?" asked McBride.

Kraft nodded. "There were no marks on it. Thing was never opened with anything but a key."

"Means it was someone she knew," said Flynt.

"Not necessarily," said Kraft.

"Could be a stranger," Cooley said as he sat down on the bed. "She could have let him in."

The clock on the window said almost four.

"Nice girl in the big city," Cooley said, as if the words were a title.

"When was she last seen?" asked Kraft.

"Looks like Monday night," McBride answered. He gave the lieutenant a rundown of the information they'd gotten. He made a special point to emphasize the story about Freddie Watson.

Kraft said they'd have to check him out and McBride said they'd already sent his name to headquarters for the computer.

The room was quiet.

"They had quite a fight here," Cooley said, remembering the scene.

"The guy that did it, he wiped the place clean," Kraft reported. "There are no prints anywhere. Definitely. And the place was ransacked."

"Is that right?" asked McBride.

Kraft nodded.

"What about her family?" Cooley asked.

"Nice people, I gather," Kraft said. "The family priest was out at their house. They took it pretty bad, I guess. She was the oldest child. Three children. Two sons. We can't talk to them for a day or two."

"Did you find any boyfriends?" one of the detectives asked Cooley and McBride.

"Nothing steady, but we got two names. She dated a pilot and a lawyer."

"Have to check them out, too," Kraft said. "There's one

good thing in all this. Headquarters is interested. Everybody's pretty upset about it. She was a schoolteacher, a nice kid, a good family, and the word is the guy has to get caught good. It's the whole thing about how girls come to New York to work and the city should at least be safe for them. The word from headquarters," he went on, "is pull in everybody to work and set up round-the-clock interviews at the precinct. Canvass the whole area. Captain Fitzgerald's putting that together now, and anybody knows anything, send 'em up to the precinct to talk. We gotta get to everyone ever knew this girl."

The telephone rang. Then it rang again.

"Answer it," somebody said.

McBride was closest. He picked up the receiver. "Hello," he said.

"Hello," said a male voice. "Is Kathy there?"

"Kathy?" McBride repeated, looking quickly at the others. "No," he said casually, as everyone listened. "She's gone out for a while."

"Do you know when she'll be back?"

"She said in an hour." McBride looked at his watch. It was 4:00. "By four thirty or five. At the latest."

"Oh." The man was silent.

"Can I take a message?" McBride asked. "Tell her who called?"

"No," the man said. "It's okay. I'll call back."

He hung up.

The officers waited. Was the caller the murderer?

The phone didn't ring again.

8

THE PHONE BOOK had said: "Cleary, K. 253 W. 72."
That had to be her.

Danny stood in a booth on the corner of Broadway and
59th, shivering. He was wearing black plastic gloves, and
he left the door open. It was dark in the booth and dark
outside in the coming night of winter. He was afraid of
being seen or overheard, by the police or an informant,
and he used the gloves so no fingerprints would be found
if the call was traced. He felt as if an electronic society, like
a horde of spiders, was closing in on him and now he
stood there dumbfounded by the man's words.

"She's gone out for a while. She'll be back in an hour."

He didn't know what to think. Maybe he was the one
who was going crazy, not Joe Willie. Was the woman dead
or alive? Had Joe Willie simply lied to him again?

9

COOLEY AND MCBRIDE sat talking to Jack Pawling.
They were back in the shadows of Tweed's, and around
the room the early evening crowd was beginning to shuffle
in.

Pawling was a young executive with a large international company, but he worked here at the bar four nights a week. He liked it and it was his way of staying in touch with the kind of life and the kind of people large international companies tend to avoid. Everybody has his way of staying human and real, he said, and this was his. He was keeping the two sides of his soul alive.

"You know what I'd like?" Cooley said. "If you'd just kind of lean back and say anything you remember about Katherine that night. There's no saying the murderer didn't pop up the next morning, God knows, but right now we're focusing on that night. Everything that happened to her. The people she talked to, and the places she went."

Pawling was quiet. Down the bar, Steve Levine was making drinks; he was more upset than anyone knew.

"Where'd you first see her?" McBride asked.

"She was sitting right here," Pawling said. "In the corner, about nine, ten o'clock. You could tell what was going on with her depending on where she sat. For instance, sometimes she sat over here in the corner and she'd read a book. A Gothic novel or a mystery, or, sometimes, a good book, like *Eleanor and Franklin,* or a Camus. If it was a bad book, then she was down, and she'd probably stay over here all night and be quiet."

"By herself?" asked Cooley.

"Very likely. But if she had a good book, then chances are in an hour or so, she'd mosey out into the middle of the bar."

"Why?" asked McBride.

"I really don't know. You'll have to ask Steve more

about that. He knew her. All I can tell you about is that night. She started out here. Drinking Johnny Walker Red. That was another sign. It meant she was looking for action. After a while," he continued, "she began to talk to people and get gregarious. Up. You know what I mean?"

Cooley brought out his notebook and Pawling identified some people she had talked to.

Then he returned to Katherine and told how she gradually moved down the bar toward the crowd at the other end near the cash register.

"And there," Cooley interjected, "Steve said she was talking to some guy he didn't know. He said you might know him."

"She was talking to some guy," Pawling agreed, "but I don't know what happened."

"Who was he?"

"I don't know. He was from out of town somewhere."

"He was sitting on the end?" Cooley asked.

"No. This guy called Rafe was on the end. A real down-and-out guy who goes around drawing pictures of people. He hangs out all over the neighborhood. Always has his drawing pad. He was on the end. Then there was this guy and his brother."

Cooley looked at the long list of names in his notebook. "Is he one of these people?" He showed Pawling the paper. The bartender studied the list and then said, "No."

Cooley took out his pen and wrote down at the bottom, "Rafe," and then, "X."

"You said he was an out-of-towner," McBride said. "How do you know?"

On the other side of the room the jukebox started playing. "And you said he was with his brother," McBride added. "What do you mean?"

"There were these two guys," Pawling explained. "I figured they were brothers because they looked alike. They came in about nine, ten, sat down here at the end. One talked to Rafe for a long time. He was the same one talked to Katherine. The other guy was older. He could have been gay. He sat there and after a while he left. The one who stayed and talked to Rafe, he told me his name was Charlie Smith. He said he was from Chicago. Here looking for a job. I even introduced him to Katherine."

"What'd he look like?" McBride asked.

"I don't remember," said Jack. "He was blond, maybe. Big . . . good-looking. I remember his brother better."

"What were they like?" asked Cooley. He crossed out the "X" and wrote in "Charlie Smith—Chicago."

"Nice guys," said Pawling. "Normal. Regular. Quiet. Not like some of the types that come in here. I never saw either one of them before. The one that stayed, I think he went across the street with the group to the Copper Hatch afterwards."

"Did he hook up with Katherine?" Cooley asked.

"If he did, I didn't see it," Pawling said. "You should talk to Rafe. He might know something more about the guy."

"How do we find Rafe?"

"I have no idea."

Cooley and McBride left.

They had a long list now. They and the other detectives would have to locate each person and interrogate him. Up near the top somewhere in terms of priority was Freddie Watson. "Charlie Smith—Chicago," on the other hand, was way down. Watson had already assaulted Katherine once. Or at least he'd gotten in a fight of some kind with her up in her apartment and she had pressed charges. The judge dismissed the charges and threw out the case, but maybe Watson was angry at her and had gone after her again.

Charlie Smith, however, was just one more person who had once talked to Katherine Cleary.

AT THE SAME TIME Wednesday the man named Joe Willie Simpson, alias Charlie Smith, alias Jack Samuels, was probably asleep.

His wife, Carole Musty, was at home in Miami with her parents. She didn't know her husband was so close. The most important thing to her right now was her belly. It was large and round and it was growing. What was inside was five months old.

Vincent and Mary Cleary and Frank, twenty-four, and Don, twenty-three, were grieving. They were in Holyoke in northern New Jersey.

Marjorie and Mercer Simpson were in Viola Camp, Illinois. Mercer was at work on a construction site outside of the town, and Marjorie was at home. She was about to take down the Christmas tree and store the ornaments in the shed out back for another year. In the living room there were bright color photographs on the table in front of the couch. They were framed in gilt from the five and dime, pictures of Fred, twenty-two, Sue Ann, eighteen, and Joe Willie and his new bride, Carole. Joe Willie was twenty-four, Carole, seventeen.

In Holyoke, the priest may have said a few words. He may have sat in the living room and talked with the family and filled in the silence with his comforting prayers, or the family doctor may have come and given Mary Cleary an injection of whatever it is that makes people sleep at times when their hearts cannot rest. Come to bed, Mary, you can't help her now. Let it go. Sleep. Sleep.

11

COOLEY SWUNG OPEN the door and walked into the Green Oaks Bar for the third time that day. It was still Wednesday. The first time he had talked to the bartender about Katherine. The second time he had shown him his list. Now it was almost midnight and the cold night wind blew in around him as he shut the door. It seemed pitch black inside, except for the light at the back on the juke-box, and he headed for the bar.

He hadn't even crossed the room, however, when the bartender gave him a high-sign, indicating that someone he wanted was back there now by the jukebox.

Who? Cooley wanted to ask. But he didn't.

Instead he loosened his scarf, opened a couple of buttons on his coat, and made his way back toward the empty stools at the end of the bar.

There was a group of people around the jukebox, some looked like bikers, others could be junkies. The women had black lines around their eyes and leftover pimples on their cheeks.

"Hey, you, mister, you a cop?" one woman asked him.

"Ya. I'm working on this murder. Heard about it?"

The woman nodded. "Gives me the shivers." She had on a yellow T-shirt.

"Don't blame you," said Cooley. "Guy's on the loose, you know. We wanna get him before he does it again."

"Again?"

"You never know," said Cooley.

"Any idea who he is?"

"No. Any of you know the girl? Katherine Cleary?"

"She hung around the neighborhood," one woman said. "Used to come in here. I'd recognize her if I saw her, but, you know, I don't know nothing about her."

"I was with her the night she died," said one of the black guys. He wore a dark skullcap and a peacoat.

Cooley looked at him. Was this Rafe? Or someone else? "Oh. Where was that?"

"Up at Tweed's. I was in there. You should talk to me," he taunted. "I might know something."

"Terrific," Cooley said with a grin. "You didn't see her with anyone, did you?"

"No. She was alone."

"You aren't by any chance the guy that draws pictures, are you? Rafe?"

The man smiled. He looked pleased.

Cooley smiled, too. You could never figure it, he thought. Sometimes you decide to do one more thing before turning in and it comes up zero and you get pissed at your job, pissed at yourself for getting so goddamned wrapped up in it, pissed you didn't go home when you had the chance. But then, other times, you get what you want. How're you supposed to know?

"You're a famous artist," Cooley said. "I even heard you were drawing pictures Monday night in Tweed's."

Rafe looked blank. "No. Not that night. I had my pad, but I wasn't in the mood."

"You saw Katherine?"

"Ya, she was there, hanging around."

"There was one guy you talked to—"

"Who says?" Rafe looked suspicious.

"We're trying to find everyone she talked to that night in Tweed's, and it seems there was one guy nobody knows—"

"Somebody must know him," the T-shirt said. "There aren't too many people come around nobody knows."

"But this guy, we can't get much on him. Nobody knows him. He was talking to Katherine for a bit there. Then he ran into her later cross the street at the Hatch. The bartender at Tweed's," Cooley went on, looking at Rafe, "said you were talking to this guy. He said you might remember more."

Rafe shook his head slowly as if trying to piece it together in his mind. "No," he said, "I don't remember. I do remember shooting the breeze with Katherine, but I wouldn't remember that if she hadn't turned up murdered. I got a bad memory. But her, that shook me up. But some stranger, don't remember that."

"Blond, young, good-looking. Said his name was Charlie Smith."

"I remember Steve Levine and a couple of others, but not this guy."

Pawling couldn't have been wrong, Cooley thought. "Bartender said you were down at the end of the bar and there was one guy and maybe his brother. Brother had glasses. Maybe he was gay and you were talking to them." Cooley paused. "Could you have forgotten?"

Rafe looked at him. "Yes," he said.

Nobody said anything for a while and Cooley thought about how the guy, who lived down so close to the ground, was being honest with him and about how he, the cop, was looking for help. It was a nice switch for a change. It wouldn't have happened if the guy hadn't liked Katherine Cleary, if she hadn't affected him inside his own oblivion.

"Will you think on it?" he asked Rafe. "I'll come back tomorrow, catch you here around nine. It might be nothing, but—"

"I catch your drift," Rafe said. "I'll put my mind to it."

12

SEVENTY-SECOND STREET is a long way from Holyoke, New Jersey.

They're separated by about thirty-five miles of city streets, marshlands, and the best way to get to Holyoke is to head west on 72nd Street.

Turn north on West End Avenue and go up past the high old brick buildings, and then head west again on 96th Street. Go north along the highway, across the George Washington Bridge, and then you are gazing, as the crow flies, toward Holyoke.

There is another route. Turn left at 72nd Street and follow the road along the Hudson River down to the Lincoln Tunnel. Then head west and go under the river to New Jersey. This takes you past the flats and the swamps and the oil refineries.

Either way, you end up about an hour and a half later out by the furniture stores. You're getting close to Holyoke and there's little to see except secondhand-car lots, glass showrooms, and gasoline stations run by high school boys.

Eventually you turn off the turnpike and leave the Mack trucks and the cross-country travelers behind. Then you get on the two-lane asphalt highways. In the old days this part of New Jersey was owned by people who kept stallions and ponies, jewels, and mansions. But back in the days when automobiles were still square and little girls always knew who they would marry, the land was sold and the people moved. They went across the river to settle in upright stone palaces in New York City.

The land turned into housing developments. Today they spread out over New Jersey like patches of material, and the place is overrun with houses, cars from Detroit, and shopping centers.

This is the part of the world where Katherine Cleary lived, but it is not where she was born. She came here as a child when her parents decided they wanted something different from Brooklyn, New York. Katherine Cleary was born in Brooklyn in 1944 in St. Thomas Aquinas's Parish. She had two parents and, for a while, she had no brothers.

When Katherine was ten her parents moved south to Queens, and then, after two years, they moved again. This time they headed west as far as New Jersey, and the suburb they chose was Holyoke.

The two-story white house is as far away as Holyoke gets from the neon signs and the smell of gasoline and trucks. Coming from New York, you turn off the asphalt at a place where a service station, a tavern, and two stores make a corner. You go past the yellow and blue and pink houses and then after a while the road begins to curve and get narrower and suddenly you are upon a piece of the old New Jersey hills.

Here is an attractive white house, and across the street is the forest, gray and pale and green, with silver trees and patches of cedar and birch and pine. This is where Katherine played and dreamed and read her books.

The Clearys had three children and Katherine was the eldest. The house had four bedrooms and two levels. It had a living room, a kitchen, crucifixes on the wall, the Holy Bible on the shelf, and one car outside in the driveway, near the front lawn and the lilac bushes. In the backyard there were more bushes and an apple tree and a barbecue stand.

Very little is known about Katherine's childhood. And the only memories that do exist are those that Katherine had and those she chose to tell her friends. Later she mentioned how much she loved to read and she pictured herself as the kind of child who read books on the bus and over dinner and even late at night when she was supposed to be asleep.

The other memory Katherine passed on to her friends was her impression she had been treated differently than she would have been if she were a boy. Those were the days when expectations for girls were still very different from those for their brothers, and Katherine used to say she remembered her mother working around the house, and that she always had to help while her younger brothers were allowed to play.

Even as daily life was going on around her, though, she would look out into the air and sky and fantasize about how life could be. There was a fantasy world there in her head, she later confided to friends, and sometimes she didn't know then—and still didn't know now—what was real and what was imaginary. She read a lot of books about women in gowns and the lovers who kissed their hands and the men who arrived at the end to protect their lives, and sometimes, she confessed, she worried whether she had confused these dreams with other more legitimate expectations. The problem was, she said, part of her really did believe this romance and security could, and should, happen to her. When they didn't, she said, she supposed it was her fault, her failure.

She didn't know what to expect or want realistically from adult life, she told Steve Levine late one night when they talked over glasses of wine. All she did know, she said, was that she wanted to be freer and more independent than her mother had been able to be.

Mary Cleary has a kind voice. It is soft and aging now and it sounds the way a mother's voice should sound. It is full of tenderness and caring. With her husband she raised three children and sent them all to college, but, most of all, as Katherine would later tell it, Mary Cleary always symbolized to her daughter the long tradition of the woman's role and the woman's service in the home. And, as Katherine understood it, this meant a woman's destiny was to get married as soon as possible and, like her mother, pass that tradition on to someone new.

That's where Katherine fit in, she maintained: Much of that tradition was supposed to be picked up and carried on by her.

Vincent Cleary, an accountant for a local insurance company in North Jersey, was fifty-nine years old the year his first-born child died. He is a tall man, and in the days when he and Mary lived in Brooklyn his face must have been handsome and strong. Now it is older and there are lines along the forehead.

"He's kind and gentle and loving," his wife said. "He's even sentimental. He just doesn't always know how to share his feelings," she added. "He holds a lot inside."

To understand Katherine Cleary you have to know

something about her body. At the end, it weighed one hundred and two pounds; in the beginning, it started out the way all bodies do, little and pink and warm.

Then it lengthened out a bit at a time in all the places where that happens and it got tiny dots of red color, the freckles of the Irish, and was soft and smooth and young.

But then it began to twist in a way that most bodies don't.

This happened about the time when little girls begin to wonder if their chests will ever swell out and perform the way they're supposed to. Katherine did begin to swell, but in the wrong places. It happened on her back.

It had a name. It was called scoliosis, from the Greek word *skoliosis,* meaning crookedness of a bodily part. When Katherine was about ten years old the right side of her back up close to her shoulder began slowly taking on a curve, a rounded aspect, as if something inside had been contained too long and was swelling out, away from its natural place. It was a lateral curvature of the spine.

Several years went by and the swelling grew and there were conversations in the family about it. Katherine wondered why she had grown that way when others did not. There was no clear explanation why, and her fantasies about her own guilt and blame began to thrive.

In time it reached the point where doctors were consulted and medical expertise solicited. Specialists said the lump on the girl's back could not be removed, but they hoped a spinal operation would fix her shoulders and make them level. Accordingly, sometime after the Clearys moved to New Jersey, Katherine went to the hospital. She was twelve or thirteen years old.

She stayed there a very long time. The surgery itself
lasted most of a day and left, according to her autopsy
report, "an eleven and one-half inch scar [running] along
the vertical column from the midscapular area to the lumbar area."

Sometime later Katherine Cleary came back to Holyoke. She was probably brought in an ambulance because
she was stretched out flat as a board in a cast that extended from her neck to the end of her toes. It was difficult
to transport her upstairs to her bedroom and it was decided instead to keep her downstairs, where she could still
be part of everything for as long as she was bedridden.

Consequently her bed was set up in the living room. It
was not far from the kitchen and the bathroom she could
not use, and for many months she lay flat on her back,
looking out across the peak of her nose at the woods
beyond the front door.

She watched the birds pecking and chirping and grew
to love the finches and the jays as if they were relatives.
Cars passed and neighbors came. A tutor arrived with
books and lessons every day. Katherine read and read,
and the difference between her life and the lives inside the
cardboard casts became greater and greater. She watched
television and ate on trays; few friends came to see her and
forever afterward she remembered the months of her ill-
ness.

The months went by and it seemed, in time, as if a shell
of aloneness was building up around her and the bed, the
way leaves pile up in the wind against a tree in the middle
of a field. She lay there in the dark and in the silent afternoons and then, little by little, the date began to approach

when she would go down to the hospital and the end would come. The cast would go and her life would begin again.

The only thing was, that wasn't the way it happened.

She did go down to the hospital and the cast came off, but then the doctors had to tell Vincent and Mary Cleary that the operation had been a failure.

Katherine's shoulders were no longer uneven, that was true, but now, for the first time, her little teenage hips were crooked. The right side was higher than the left.

Forever after Katherine would limp when she walked and assume with almost every waking breath that people were looking in disgust at her twisted body. The greatest secret she could ever share would be her contempt for her own flesh and her deepest pain, the confusion that brought.

It was a hard time for the family.

Katherine went to church for the first time in months, and the sounds of Latin and pipes, the priests intoning against sin and evil, moved over her with the soothing comfort of a balm. She was caught up in the ritual of the incense and the gold, the wafers and the Hail Marys, but she also felt bewildered. The change from her long flat bed was too great. The Church said she belonged and said there was faith and goodness in worship and she could share it. But she was genuinely perplexed.

Was she going to be a cripple or a woman—and what was the difference?

The priests spoke of Jesus Christ and God and suggested everything was all His doing. But she had her doubts. Why give God the responsibility, when she could take it? She would later talk of psychology and say she was "doomed." The Church pictured heaven and hell as spots in the future, but Katherine came to think she was already there. And she had been shut up in fifty pounds of plaster for a year and it hadn't done any good. Why did it have to happen? Why her? The priests had some goddamn nerve talking about Christ when her life was ruined. What about me? What about Katherine? What's going to happen to her? It made her so goddamn mad it made her so Jesus Christ goddamn bitch mad. What in Christ was going to happen to her?

13

WHEN KATHERINE WAS murdered, many of her friends refused to talk about her. They would not reveal her age, her job, the date of her birth, or even her middle name. They said they did not want to hurt her parents, but they also implied they were protecting Katherine from some terrible slander. They refused, they said, to turn her life into material for talk and gossip or to help in any way, as they saw it, to destroy the dignity she had. One even got hysterical and shrieked that Katherine's death had destroyed *her* life as well, as if a common germ had afflicted them both, but only one, she, had been permitted to survive.

The Clearys, too, did not want to talk to outsiders about their daughter. Three years later one of their sons got married. And in the weeks before the wedding Vincent and Mary finally opened up the closet where "Katherine's things" had long been stored. They took down the boxes and looked through the diplomas and the letters, the old birthday cards and the yearbooks.

And then Mary turned to Vincent and said, "Why are we keeping these?" And he said he didn't know, and she said she didn't know either. But they were keeping the boxes the way you keep a lock of hair or a photograph that curls along the edges and turns yellow.

"We just threw out her things last week," Mary told a friend. "We still feel very badly about her and we miss her all the time, but I feel she's happy now." There was a pause in the conversation and then she said, "I think I've learned to get along, and spiritually I know Katherine is at peace now.

"In everyone's death there is guilt," she said, "but in time you realize you must forgive and let your life go on. Not to," she said, "to me is a sin.

"I don't nag myself," she added. "I've given up the guilt. Guilt is the saddest word in the dictionary."

As one of their sons said in a brief telephone conversation soon after the murder: "She only told my parents the good things. And they shouldn't have to know what they know now. They'll never get over it. They'll never be the same again. They don't want to talk to anyone about it."

14

JOE WILLIE SIMPSON, the man no one remembered on the most important night of his life, started out a long way from bars and subways and the rolling sound of empty trash cans. He came from a place far beyond the New York streets and the New Jersey hills.

Illinois is low and flat. It has steel mills and industrial plants in the north and the rest of the state is rolling prairie land that stretches for miles in all directions. This is where Joe Willie lived. His home was southwest of Springfield, in Clay County, where the Little Wabash River lies.

Clay County is the kind of place where the summer heat is so intense even the sugar flies seem to mosey along at half speed. The heat sets in around the middle of May and doesn't let up until October. And then the winter starts, winter so fierce and ruinous it spreads over the land like an avalanche. The snow and the ice cover the ground hard, as if to smother it, and the wind attacks from the side.

In summer, though, the land is brown and yellow and green. There are sycamore and elm, full with leaves; corn that is tall and gold by mid-August; and creeks where the crawdads crawl. The fields have bugs and snakes and there are even birds' nests, round and made of twigs, stuck in down close to the ground.

Joseph William Simpson was born November 3, 1949, in Viola Camp, Illinois. He was to be called Joe Willie.

Viola Camp, with a population of twenty thousand today, has a small central square, a traffic light, and a mortuary made of bricks and white paint. Out beyond the square there are more streets and houses and stores, but none of the buildings are more than two stories tall and they are all colored white. There are screens in the windows to keep out the flies, fans on the ceiling, and the doors are left unlocked at night.

Three blocks from the center of town is a narrow street just wide enough for cars to park on both sides and another car to pass in the middle. Here there is a small white clapboard house with a pointed roof and little windows, a narrow porch in front and a tulip tree in back. It is two feet from the sidewalk, and through the years it has acquired the same weather-beaten look as the other houses on the block.

This is the spot where the Simpson family has lived and grown for the last thirty years.

In 1916 Mercer Simpson, the head of the family, was born out on the county land in "a little bitty town" with twelve buildings and a feed house. Later, as a young man, he moved to Viola Camp and has lived there ever since, but he still looks country.

The furrows on his face are deep and the vessels along his hands are high, reminders somehow of the harsh, principled beliefs that tie him to the earth. He often looks down at them, spread out flat and straight before his eyes, and studies the lines there as if to find either information or relief. He is a silent man, at least in public, and this is a gesture of his, the pulling out of his hands and looking down, the way other people scratch their heads or bite their fingernails. It seems to give him time and something to do.

Mr. Simpson worked as a heavy-equipment operator for a private contractor outside of town and he wore dark-green coveralls with the look of dust and powder to them. He used to run the machinery and come home at night with the sounds still ringing in his ears. In 1972 he was made foreman of the work gang.

Mrs. Simpson now works as a clerk in the local bank and she leaves home about nine in the morning. In all the years when her three children were little, however, she stayed at home and worked all day long and into the night caring for them and her husband.

The house is dark and still and there is a feeling here of what became of the eldest son. It is as if the darkness whispers and the stillness speaks. They do not, of course, but the feeling remains, as if somebody—Joe Willie—got lost here once and his body was never found.

The windows are small and far apart and the only bright place in the house is the kitchen, where there is red oilcloth on the table and a loaf of Wonder Bread on the shelf. Sun shines in the west window and out beyond the steps are a lawn, a shed and a tulip tree. "That tree always reminds me of Joe Willie," Marjorie Simpson said one day. "It starts out real thin and then it spreads out full around the middle with flowers and blossoms and then it begins to taper off at the top."

The tree itself blows in the wind and seems misplaced, a seed deposited there by accident and left to grow as best it could. It has long velvet petals, lips that are lush and lovely, and is pretty and rich, unlike the rest of the dry expanse of lawn.

Back inside there are five rooms and two floors and perhaps no doors except those at the front and at the back and on the bathroom. The rooms all seem to blend from one to another with no separation point in between except, maybe, a long hanging piece of faded cloth.

Downstairs, by the street, are the living room and the Simpsons' bedroom. In the middle, in what might be a hall, is a bedroom; beyond that, the kitchen. From the bedroom a steep, narrow staircase leads up to a tiny room that used to be the attic but was converted into a bedroom for Joe Willie and his brother, Fred. The ceiling slopes down low like a four-cornered hat and the walls are so close together you can almost reach from one side to the other.

The house is still and neat. There are no dirty dishes in the sink, no pots on the stove, no clothes lying misplaced. It's the kind of house where the bedrooms are not just for sleeping but for storage, too, and there are boxes under the beds—carton boxes and metal boxes, boxes bulging with winter clothes in the summer and summer clothes in the winter, with belongings that are too precious or too sorry for daily use. The place feels like an impacted wisdom tooth: There is pain because there is so much beneath the surface.

The living room is square and crowded with chairs bought through the years to accommodate an increasing number of people. Faded greens and reds, they are lined up along the walls, each a different size and shape. They all face the middle, where another chair sits. It is straight-backed and wooden, without foam or cushions. This is Mrs. Simpson's chair.

She is a short woman with brown hair and ample breasts. In the summer she wears cotton dresses with small prints of flowers, and in the winter she wears skirts and sweaters. Her husband is tall and thin. They are both handsome and sturdy-looking, as if they come from good, principled stock.

After the lawyer appointed by the courts to represent their eldest son flew to Indianapolis to see them, he described them as "American Gothic." They met him at the airport and drove him to a small diner where they ordered coffee and doughnuts, and talked. Afterward, he returned to New York City. They reminded him of the painting by Grant Wood, he said—of the man and woman, stern and severe, she with her hair parted in the middle and pulled back tight, he with a pitchfork in his hands. There was a barn at their backs and all kinds of adversity and determination in their lives.

But the Simpsons are not like that. They are not so stern or grim or determined. But most of all, they are not so barren. There is something of that lush, overgrown, and yet still secretive sense of the Midwest about them and their lives.

This is a place, the Midwest, where people came with all their dreams. They came by wagon and by train and up the river, and they got the Land, rich and fertile and as full of promise as their dreams. And this sense of anticipation, as well as the disappointment and resentment it brings, is part of the Simpsons and their legacy to their son.

It's as if they all had a plan here, years ago, some pact among the Simpsons, and it went awry. Today no one mentions it anymore, as if, maybe, whatever it was has even been forgotten. And yet it lingers, the scent of lost promise. This is the Midwest here in Viola Camp. The colors are faded and the screen door in front doesn't quite shut. In the near silence of a sweltering summer afternoon, the sounds of cars and distant voices drift in like the faint buzz of moths, and you hear the telephone ring in the house next door.

There is a four-lane highway here, but it goes by outside of town without stopping. There are hot dog stands and root beer joints, but they don't have national names, and there are factories, but all they make is brown paper bags. The streets run in parallel lines and head straight back out to the fields, and the one movie theater in town shuts down in the summer when the drive-in opens with the coming heat.

Life has been hard for the Simpsons. There is a community of life here in this town and surely the Simpsons are part of it, but it seems as if a long dirt road stretches between them and the house next door. It is hard to imagine them talking on the telephone, or spending New Year's Eve anywhere but at home. Life has been just too hard and work too long.

They are not churchgoing anymore and say they have forgotten much of the Baptist teachings they once knew. But they admit to a stern Christian sense of life and have their rules for this and their rules for that, and there is a lot that is not sanctioned. They've tried hard to make the best of what they had, they say, and if life has filled them with a deep distrust of the wealthy and the privileged, they would say this is the way it's got to be because no one's going to look out for us but ourselves.

They would also say, in a sad but proud, guilt-free way, that if, by chance, one amongst them drifted out too far on his own, in his own peculiar silent ways, then that's terrible but that's just the way it was.

"There's only so much time and so much energy," Mrs. Simpson said once. "I did everything I could but there just wasn't always enough to go around."

She was talking at home one Sunday afternoon in the middle of summer. It was hot and the flies were buzzing. The days had long passed since the story of her son and Katherine Cleary covered the front pages.

Daniel P. Murray was there, as he often is, talking to Mrs. Simpson, spending time with her husband, and this time the talk was about Joe Willie.

The living room was dark. The shades were drawn to keep out the heat. Mr. Simpson was sitting in a rocking chair in the far corner. Mrs. Simpson pulled her chair out into the center of the room. Sue Ann was there but she never said a word. Fred was up north in Springfield, where he lived.

Marjorie Simpson did most of the talking. She spoke about homemade pie and blizzards, the cost of land and the heat of the day, and then suddenly she said, "He shouldn't have hurt that girl, but if anything more bad is said about him in the newspapers, I just don't think I can take it. I just don't think he deserves any more. He's a good boy, a real fine boy."

Mercer Simpson, in dusty overalls and short-cropped

hair, leaned back in his rocking chair in the corner. He said he agreed and then he lapsed into silence.

"Joe Willie was a perfect child," Marjorie Simpson said. "We never had any trouble with him."

And then she went on. He was a quiet boy, she said. He never cried much and he never did show too many of his feelings, never, since the very beginning. If he got a bee sting, he'd try to hide it, or if he skinned his arm, he'd never say anything. Once he even fell down out back in the yard and he came in through the screen door and stood in the kitchen with his arm held out in front.

There was blood dripping down and he had a real bad cut, not real real bad, she said, but it was enough to make a person hurt and cry. But Joe Willie, he didn't cry, he didn't even say it hurt. In fact, he said it didn't hurt. He stood there and she fixed it with water and the red Mercurochrome and you know how that hurts, but he stood there with his yellow hair and strong little body, the arm with the cut held up high by the other arm.

That's the way he was, strong, quiet, serious, and good.

She talked on and on and the picture of Joe Willie Simpson began to come alive. Her voice was slow and inflected with traces of the Midwest around the vowels and the rhythm. All the while her husband sat in the corner and listened, hard, close, and it seemed as if he was keeping track and saving, perhaps, his comment for later, in private.

The way Marjorie told it, three things had always been true about Joe Willie. He liked to be alone and he liked to make plans and he liked things that didn't talk. As a child he would spend a lot of time by himself either up in his attic room or out on the lawn. Later, when he was about eight, he began to go out by himself to the creek that ran through the fields on the outside of town. After school or on weekends, he would say, "Please, please," and sooner or later his father and mother would say "Okay," and take him in the car and leave him off. He'd stand there in the road and watch the car turn around and head back toward town, and then he'd go off somewhere by himself.

He walked to the creek and lay on his stomach on the edge and hunted for crawdads in the water beneath the rocks. When he caught them, he let them wriggle in his hands for a while and then he dropped them back. Every now and then, he'd bring one home, but he said he didn't really care about catching them. He didn't want to kill them, he said; he just liked to watch them.

Other times his parents would take him out to the railroad tracks in another part of the fields and after they were gone he'd walk up and down and sometimes head out into the corn and alfalfa looking for rabbits and bugs. Sometimes, they said, when they came back just before the sun went down, they would find him lying on his back in the grass staring up at the sky.

Sometimes, though, they wouldn't find him at all. They would drive around for a while looking. "Joe Willie," they'd call into the coming darkness, "Joe Willie."

And then he'd show up somewhere and they'd stop the car, open the door, and let him in.

"Where've you been?" they'd say. "I declare, I don't know what gets into you sometimes."

And Joe Willie would look out across the fields, as if

maybe he knew and maybe he didn't know but that the answer might lie way over there somewhere where the darkening sky was coming across the land like a nearing storm.

Marjorie Simpson and her husband never did say if he had a friend. They just said he liked animals and he liked to be alone.

At home he looked at magazines and cereal boxes and he was always cutting along the dotted lines to send away for free books and pamphlets.

"Mom," he'd say, "can I have a stamp?"

"What for?"

"I want to send for this," he'd say, and it'd be for information on a cruise to Curaçao or the Inns of the British Isles, Extinct Species, or How to Take Care of Your Pet.

"But you're not going to the British Isles," she'd say.

"I know."

"Then why do you want that book?"

"Just because."

As time went on, he became interested in all kinds of animals, especially dinosaurs and prehistoric creatures. He got on the mailing list of the American Museum of Natural History in New York City and owned, variously, dogs, cats, rabbits, hamsters, and even the iguana Danny bought him. "I love animals," he told Danny, "because you always know where you are with them. With people you never know."

The way his parents explain it, Joe Willie was always "perfect" and "normal" these early years. He had no emotional problems. He never withdrew or seemed out of touch with reality, and there was nothing in his lonely, silent perusal of the world that disturbed them. They may be right; they may not. Danny, for one, never agreed with them.

According to their way of thinking, everything started in 1960 when he was hit by a car. He was ten years old and he was a traffic-patrol boy on the street outside of school. One afternoon a car struck him in the side and he was knocked unconscious for several seconds. He was taken to the doctor for examination, but the doctor found no sign of a concussion or injuries, only a bruise.

Afterward, though, the Simpsons maintain, the quality of Joe Willie's mind changed. He began to forget things and his awareness seemed to drift in and out like a kite moving off on different winds. He began to experience pains in his head, go into a state of confusion sometimes, and choke so hard he could not talk or breathe.

These may have been symptoms brought on by earlier conditions, but Marjorie and Mercer would tell each other it was due to the car accident. Even to this day, they speak with anger and bitterness about the driver. "She was a rich woman in town," who never bothered to call and ask how the boy was doing. "She didn't even have a license to drive," Marjorie said, "and she still didn't get a ticket or nothing."

At this time Joe Willie had a pet rabbit, and little things that happened with the rabbit were an example, Mrs. Simpson said, of what had gone wrong with Joe Willie.

"He always put this rabbit out in the yard to go, but now what happened was, he'd forget it. After a while, I'd be in the kitchen and I'd say, 'Joe Willie, go bring the rabbit in,' and he'd say, 'I already did,' and I'd say, 'No, you didn't.' "

And then after a while Joe Willie would miss the rabbit

and he'd go push open the screen door and go out into the backyard to see if it was there. He'd walk around looking for it and then find it, grazing quietly somewhere near the shed or the fence at the back. Joe Willie would sit down on the grass and let the animal nibble his fingers. He'd pet him, feel his warm belly, and look up at the stars. Then, after a while, he'd bring him back inside.

Thinking back on those early days, however, nobody remembered if Joe Willie was ever tense or upset. Even later, when the trouble did start, nobody perceived him as a psychological composition; it was as if everything was contracted from a germ.

They did tell a story, however, about the night the family kitten was meowing in the yard.

Joe Willie and Fred were upstairs in their attic room. It was cold, winter or late autumn, and it was past midnight. Then, just below their little window overlooking the house next door and the corridor in between, a kitten began to meow.

The animal was alone, separated from the rest of the litter, and it bleated a lonely sound and was frightened by the dark and silence.

Upstairs Joe Willie listened.

The kitten went on and on and after a while Joe Willie yelled out at it to shut up. He kept yelling at the animal and then suddenly he got up and leaned his head out the window into the darkness.

"Shut up, cat," he screamed.

He got back into bed and tried to go to sleep, but the noise continued. Then all of a sudden he reached out, picked up the alarm clock by the bed, and pitched it out the window into the night.

The kitten shrieked and shrieked once more, and then the howling stopped. Joe Willie lay on his bed for a while, staring up at the ceiling checkered with pictures of dinosaurs and lizards and mountain lions, and then he drifted off to sleep.

Next morning he came down for breakfast. "D'you hear that kitten last night?" he said to his mother. "Drove me crazy; I couldn't sleep."

After a while he went outside and walked over to the spot where the noise had come from.

He found the kitten lying on the cold hard ground of winter. Its legs were sticking straight up in the air.

Joe Willie was stunned. He stood over the little body and then tears began to collect in his eyes and he started to cry. He kicked at the ground, and then he kicked again and again and then he kicked hard at the body of the kitten. The animal didn't go very far, but Joe Willie went over and sat down beside it, leaning up against the side of the house. He was quiet for a long time. He reached out to pick up the clock and he sat there in silence, turning the weapon over and over in his hands.

It was his only violent act until the murder, almost fifteen years later.

At that point in the conversation Mrs. Simpson started to cry. The tears had been welling up and now they began to seep over the sides. "I'm not ashamed by what happened with the schoolteacher," she said, the tears trickling down her face. "I just feel bad.

"He always wanted a good life, but things went wrong for him from the very beginning. We did the best we could with him, but there comes a time," she said, "when you can only go so far. I've always tried to do the best, but I'm sure I haven't always done right."

There's a story she tells, for example.

She took Joe Willie to the hospital to have a checkup when he was three years old. The little boy was sitting on the wide car seat beside her, held in by a shoulder strap that tucked in on the bottom underneath his fanny.

"Where are we going?" he asked.

His mother looked over at him. "I've had you a long time," she teased, "and I'm tired of you. It's time to turn you in."

Joe Willie began to cry, slowly at first, so his mother didn't think much of it. Then he began to cry harder and harder.

"Hush up," she said kindly, patting him on the head. "I was only teasing. I didn't mean anything bad."

THE MEDICAL RECORDS are eleven inches long, eight inches wide, and they stand about one and one-half inches high. They start back close to the beginning, in the days when Joe Willie had nothing but an occasional cold and tonsillitis. In time, however, the single-spaced typewritten sheets begin to talk about far more serious things, and from the time he was twelve years old they suggest the kind of drama that later took him out to 72nd Street. The records end, abruptly, when he was sixteen.

The earliest are signed by family doctors, the kind of gentle people who live in small towns and have an office on the main square with one woman to help out as nurse and secretary. In these Joe Willie is called "Joey" and "the boy." Later, however, all the doctors are specialists; "Joey" is "the patient," and the records shift noticeably from a concentration on the boy alone to a broad and highly detailed picture of the Simpson family as a whole.

They talk about Mr. Simpson's job, how much money the family had, and whether the house was mortgaged. They probe the relationships in the little household and they go on at length about the two parents, who are referred to periodically as the "domineering mother" and the "absent father."

Mrs. Simpson, the records claim, "makes most of the patient's decisions." After a long office visit, one doctor wrote:

> She spoke only of how she had talked with the boy and helped him make decisions and how she calmed him down. There was no mention of any involvement on the part of the patient's father. When questioned regarding this, she stated that the patient and his father were very close, but, naturally, that since Mr. Simpson had to go to work every day, he did not have the time to devote to the patient.

The doctor said he tried to question her more closely about Joe Willie's "relationship with his father and the time they spent together," but, he said, "she appeared to be resentful and repeatedly brushed the questions aside."

She was, the records say repeatedly, "a good person." They emphasize, though, that she was "tense and anxious." She suffered from such severe migraines that Joe

Willie had "to assume responsibilities for the younger children." She said life was "hard" and that there was not enough money to pay for Joe Willie's medical bills and, indeed, there was not. One year there was only $5,000 for five people; another year, $5,500; another, $6,000.

The records speak less of Mercer Simpson. They say, in fact, that the responsibility for dealing with "the patient," both at home and with the doctors, fell to the mother. Mr. Simpson seldom visited the doctors and when he did, they wrote, he came in his work overalls, and sat in silence. They say he rarely talked during these sessions and might, frequently, utter no more than two or three words. He, too, though, the doctors emphasized, was "a good man." He had to work so long and hard he couldn't give as much attention to his son's activities and interests as he wanted.

"The patient," they observe, "expressed resentment at his father's absence." He, too, the doctors wrote, "speaks little" and when he does, says he "doesn't feel much" or "can't remember." He is described as "cooperative," "very intelligent," and "pleasant," but he admits to not sleeping well and says he wants to "get away" to avoid pressures at home.

The first medical records of any significance about Joe Willie are dated November 20, 1962, seventeen days after Joe Willie's thirteenth birthday. Joe Willie was in the seventh grade and that year he would get eighty-four in arithmetic, eighty-six in geography and history, and ninety in music, physical education, and English.

On November twentieth Joe Willie and his mother went to see a bone specialist and a radiologist about a severe pain Joe Willie had in his right leg. It was an important matter.

The records of these two visits and others that followed during the next two months are precise medically, but, interestingly, apparently the Simpsons never confided in the doctors then about what was going on simultaneously inside the family. That was only revealed to the doctors several years later, during the course of another problem.

It happened that Joe Willie had been a member of the local boys' club since he was seven years old. It is not clear what this organization did, except, presumably, organize baseball games and have picnics, but they did have a club-house. And sometime in 1961 Joe Willie got a part-time job there cutting the grass. He went after school and on Saturdays and earned a few dollars a week to supplement the very small allowance his family could afford to give him.

Then, sometime in 1962, when he was twelve, Joe Willie joined the Boy Scouts as well. He now had membership in two clubs, but in the new one he quickly gained the rank of First-Class Scout and was so popular with the other boys that he was elected the Scout Leader. This was Joe Willie's second experience at any kind of leadership role. The first, as a patrol boy, had ended two years earlier when he was hit by the car.

This one ended too, in September 1962.

The medical records two years later say that for some unexplained reason a conflict developed that fall in the family over whether Joe Willie should belong to two clubs. It seems his commitment to the Scouts was jeopardizing his part-time job with the other club. Finally, in September 1962, "he gave up his Scouting career."

The "selection," the reporter maintains, "was a decision directed by his mother."

This episode is the first hint in the pages and pages of records that there had ever been any disappointment in the boy's life, and sometime within the next few weeks after it happened, he ran away from home for the first time.

It happened after school one day. His mother went to look for him in the yard and he wasn't there. She looked upstairs and out in the street, but there was no sign of him. When Mr. Simpson came home he suggested maybe Joe Willie had gone to the fields outside of town.

They got in the car and drove out by the creek and the railroad tracks. There was no sign of him. They called and called, but there was no answer.

Finally they saw him hiding in a cornfield.

"Joe Willie, you come here," his mother called.

The boy didn't move.

"Come on, Joe Willie. It's time to go home now. Come on," she said, "I'm telling you."

Finally the boy came. He didn't say a word. He climbed in the back seat of the car and they went home.

Later, at home, Joe Willie began to complain of headaches, and Mrs. Simpson took him to the doctor. She explained about what was referred to as Joe Willie's "nervousness." The doctor prescribed a drug called Dilantin, a general depressant of the central nervous system used to control excessive tension and excitability. It was supposed to calm the boy and control the headaches. This alone—a reference to headaches and the nervousness—was in the records of the time. There was nothing about running away.

Several weeks later Joe Willie took off again. This time

his parents found him walking in the fields, headed away
from home.

He ran away one more time that fall, and then on Sunday, November 11, Joe Willie woke up with a severe pain
in his right foot. He tried to move it, but an excruciating
pain flared all the way up the leg.

"Hey, Mom," he called downstairs.

"What?"

"My foot."

"What about it?"

"It hurts."

He stayed in bed that day and the next, and after a while
the pain gradually moved out of the area of the foot and
started climbing up the leg.

Mrs. Simpson called the family doctor. He said Joe Willie should get bed rest, but when that didn't work, he
referred them to a bone specialist and radiologist.

The two appointments were for November 20, and afterward the bone specialist wrote:

> Comes to the office because of pain in his right foot.
> Learned this was present when he awakened Sunday morn-
> ing ten days ago. On the Saturday before he had gone for
> an hour or so on a hunting expedition with his father but
> had sustained no injury. The father shot two rabbits.
>
> He has had no unusual accidents, injuries or activities of
> any sort. The pain occurred for no known reason. He has
> not been able to bear his weight comfortably on his foot
> since then. He has missed a full week of school.
>
> He is able to walk on tiptoe. He complains of a pain all
> the way from his foot up to his knee. The leg and foot
> below the knee are stone cold.

There is no complaint or abnormality in the bar or the hip or the thigh.

The X-ray report was brief:

The lower lumbar vertebrae appear normal, with no evidence of compression fracture or other injury. The joint spaces are normal and the sacroiliac joints are clear. There is no evidence of any other bone abnormality.

In the next few weeks Joe Willie was sent to see other specialists to examine the possibility of a twisted disc, a tumor, or a neurological problem. All the results were negative. There is never a hint, however, that he was faking the pain or that the pain was not severe, but simply that the cause was mysterious. There is no indication that anyone at the time wondered if the pain had a psychological origin.

Many years later, in hindsight, a psychiatrist called it "psychological hysteria," and "psychologically induced paralysis." In the light of what happened to Joe Willie afterward, he said, he could theorize that it emanated from the unconscious mind of a young boy so full of anger and repression that he was afraid of his own powers. The pain was designed, the doctor said, to keep him under control and to prevent him from running away or doing anything dangerous with the anger. At the time, however, Joe Willie is not known to have ever seen a psychiatrist.

By December, Joe Willie couldn't walk except with crutches; the leg was always cold to the touch, and numb. He had missed one month of school. He was admitted briefly to the hospital for examination and there one doctor wrote:

> The patient is a well-developed, well-nourished white male. He is alert and oriented, but quite overly apprehensive. He has admittedly been "nervous" some length of time before the onset of this illness. He has been on medication for this since September of this year. The parents and the boy are somewhat reticent to talk about the problem of these spells of nervousness.

The paralysis continued through December. Christmas came and went. Then New Year's. And then one day Mercer and Marjorie Simpson piled the children into the car and drove to a friend's house in the country for the day. The frost glistened, the air was pure. The adults sat inside around the kitchen stove and the children stayed outside to play.

After a while the other children ran across the snow to skate on the river that flowed through the farm, and Joe Willie followed. He slipped along on his crutches but he made it to the ice.

Out there something happened. He put down his crutches, put on a pair of skates and he skated out on the river ice as if nothing was the matter.

And, in fact, whatever had been the matter was over. The paralysis had ended.

In time, however, Joe Willie began to run away again. No one kept track of how many times it happened. The journeys lasted from several hours to several days and he often left as much as twice a month. Sometimes he took off from school and once he left about noon and ended up

at two o'clock the next morning in a farmhouse way out
in the country.

He knocked on the door. The watchdogs were barking
and snow was falling. The temperature had fallen below
freezing and Joe Willie had no galoshes or mittens.

An old man and woman came to the door. Joe Willie
was standing there in the dark, shivering. They brought
him inside and gave him some cocoa. After a while he
telephoned Viola Camp.

Other times Joe Willie did not leave home suddenly or
without warning. Instead, quite the opposite. He would
start packing days ahead of time. It would begin when he
would ask for a paper bag. His mother would give him one
and he'd take it upstairs to the attic and over the next few
days he would pack his toothbrush, socks, clean under-
wear. He would leave the package on the bed and make
no secret of his preparations.

Sometimes, Mrs. Simpson said later, she would climb to
the top of the stairs and try to talk him out of leaving.
Other times she would ignore him altogether. "It was,"
she told the doctors, "a ploy to get attention."

Subsequent childhood records that look back over this
earlier period say that he continued to be plagued with
severe headaches and occasional choking fits. He would
often lie awake at night for hours, and dream fitfully when
he slept. He frequently came to his mother and said he'd
had a bad dream. The records also say he masturbated like
"a normal teenager."

One notation said Mrs. Simpson "stated that the patient
had indicated some interest in girls." He was now fourteen years old. "He has telephoned them but has made no

dates." Neither she nor her husband, the report continues, "would state that the patient had been preoccupied with sex in any way."

It goes on:

> The informant stated that the patient was interested in music, football, basketball, and putting models together. The mother reported that the patient has recently expressed his desire to learn how to dance. "He also wants to smoke and drive a car," she said. "He thinks that that means everything."

This doctor described Mrs. Simpson at some length.

> She evidenced little anxiety throughout the interview. She seemed to be accustomed to the giving out of information concerning her son. Mrs. Simpson did most of the talking. The patient's father interjected only two or three times throughout the whole interview.
> The patient's mother answered questions readily enough, however her answers seemed somewhat practiced.

Then, in the spring of 1964, Joe Willie and two friends stole $10.50 from the Boys' Club. Afterward they divided the money and Joe Willie took his share and, without saying a word to anyone, went to the bus station.

It was a warm day. School would be over in several weeks, and he bought a one-way ticket to Urbana, Illinois. It was not a long ride. He sat in the back of the bus and looked out the window at the fields and streams and small towns.

When the bus pulled into Urbana, he got out and

walked around. He bought a hot dog and a Coke, and the sun began to set. His three dollars were almost gone, and something began to happen to Joe Willie Simpson.

He may have felt guilty and been struck by remorse. He may simply have realized he had no more money and no way to get any farther.

All that anyone knows is that late that afternoon, in Urbana, Illinois, Joe Willie Simpson went to the sheriff's office, confessed to his robbery of $10.50, and called his parents. They made the several hours trip to pick him up, went back to Viola Camp, and there he went to the authorities.

His trial in the local juvenile court came on August twenty-first. The judge placed him on probation and stipulated that he report once a month to his probation officer, go to church once a week, obey a nine-o'clock curfew, and "watch the association of his friends."

Joe Willie agreed.

Three days later, however, he stole some money from his mother and his brother, Fred, slipped behind the seat of the family car, and took off southwest toward Iowa.

He was gone for two days and two nights, and then on the third day, the brakes on the car failed and he pulled into a filling station. A policeman there noticed him. "How old are you, son?" he said.

Joe Willie looked him in the eye. "I'm only fourteen," he said, as the medical records quote Mrs. Simpson as saying the policeman told her. "I'm too young to drive."

When Joe Willie came home that time the Simpsons were very upset and discouraged about the whole situation. He had broken his probation and proved himself unreliable. They decided he needed another kind of medical treatment and to their way of thinking, hospitalization was the answer.

They then began another round of sessions with the medical community. Now for the first time they sought help from psychiatrists, in an effort to get the fourteen-year-old boy committed to a mental institution.

"I know he understood," Mrs. Simpson said years later as the flies circled slowly in the hot afternoon and her husband rocked in his chair. "He knew it weren't because we didn't love him or anything. We just had to, that's all. I couldn't take it anymore, with the other children and all. I just had to get him off my mind and that was the only way to do it."

Psychiatrists and juvenile authorities agreed that Joe Willie needed hospital supervision and that he wouldn't "improve" under normal living conditions. One psychiatrist, recommending that Joe Willie be admitted to a local children's hospital, said he was in a state of serious "emotional turmoil." Although the boy seemed "bland and free of overt anxiety," he wrote, the matter was "urgent."

> The parents [he added] wanted reassurance that he would not act out and hurt someone before he got in a hospital. I could not, of course, give them any real assurance and told them they would just have to watch him as best they could.

In the meantime the doctor prescribed two tranquilizers for Joe Willie "to slow him down."

Another psychiatrist was much more alarming: "The

patient," he wrote, "seems to be having progressively more difficulty handling his hostile, angry impulses." The way he read the boy's history of acting out, he said, symptoms of this antisocial behavior had first begun to appear two years ago when he started running away from home and to experience physical paralysis.

> When faced with stress and his aggressive impulses [he wrote] his main form of defense at the present time is running away. He feels if he is unable to do this he may actually harm someone in the future. He feels himself unable to handle these impulses at the present time and seems to be getting progressively worse.

It began September twenty-eighth. Marjorie Simpson picked Joe Willie up at school in the car. He was in the eighth grade now. He did not know the purpose of all his visits to the doctors except that there was something wrong with him that made him run away from home and be bad. He was the television set or the car that repeatedly turns up in the shop for repairs. He was bad property, badly put together, and badly operated.

In the beginning he didn't know the ride in the car that day was any different from any others.

"Where are we going?" he asked after a while.

"We're moving," his mother told him. "We're going to our new home." Then she took him to the hospital for commitment.

The two psychiatrists had recommended that Joe Willie be assigned to a children's hospital. Instead he was committed to a regional state institution for the mentally ill, forty miles away. This was because he was considered a "chronic runaway" and as such deemed unfit for "an environment" without so-called external controls.

At the hospital he was placed under maximum-security precautions and assigned to the adult ward with a twenty-four-hour guard.

He spent the next three months in a bed thirty-six inches wide and seventy-two inches long. There were forty-eight other beds in the room, all full of men in their forties and fifties, and for exercise he walked up and down the corridor outside.

There are a lot of records dating from this period. They talk about his need for "a temporary father figure" and they describe him as having "feelings of insecurity and inferiority." They also talk about regular doses of tranquilizers like Stelazine and Valium but they never mention that Joe Willie had therapy or was treated by a psychiatrist.

16

IN DECEMBER JOE Willie was released.

He returned to the ninth grade. He was ashamed of where he'd been, but at first he did well in school and even joined the track team. After a few weeks, though, he developed severe blisters on his feet and he quit. His marks went steadily downhill. According to the record, however, his parents congratulated the doctors and said they were "pleased" with his improvement. The home atmosphere was "better now," they said. "Joe Willie was more congenial and 'doing better.' "

Joe Willie's explanation of this period was different. It turned out, according to later records, that he was frightened. He didn't know what was happening to him. He had headaches and bad dreams and suddenly, before he'd know it, he'd find himself on the road outside of town headed north.

"I'm getting worse, Mom," he said. "I'm getting worse."

He told her he was bad and couldn't stop wanting to run away.

"Oh, Joe Willie, don't worry about it. You're fine now."

She later confided in the doctors how these were efforts on his part to get attention.

"But, Mom, I keep having these awful dreams. I keep dreaming I'm running away and that I'm gonna commit suicide."

"You're not going to commit suicide, Joe Willie, and everyone has nightmares. You're all better," she said kindly. "Don't get so excited. You've just had a lot of experiences and you need to get them straight in your head."

It was early evening and her husband wasn't home yet. She told the doctors about it later. Joe Willie'd kept saying he thought he was two people.

"There's two sides," he said. "One gets angry and the other doesn't. One loves it here and my home and you and my dad, but the other just wants to get away. And I don't know what it means. Sometimes I can't stop myself. I'm afraid, Mom," he said, his voice getting hushed and secretive. "Sometimes I'm afraid one side will take over and I'll have no control left."

Not long afterward Joe Willie had a girlfriend for the first time. Her name was Louise and she was tall and dark and her hair was high on her head and teased with a comb. Sometimes they'd meet after school and other days he'd slip out after dinner and meet her in the dark. But his parents did not like it. They did not like the girl and they were worried about Joe Willie.

"Joe Willie, why do you go out with that girl?" his mother said. "She's not from a good family," his mother continued, and he could do so much better. Besides, she added, his work at school was slipping.

In February the relationship ended and the medical records say why. "The mother stated she talked to the patient about his girlfriend, and they agreed that since he could not handle his own problems, he should not become involved with a girl who had problems too. Informant emphasized the fact that she left the decision up to the patient and he stopped dating this girl of his own accord. It was quite evident," the doctor added, "that one factor about this girl the informant did not like was the social standing of her family.

"Since breaking up with the girl," the records continued, "the patient has not dated. Informant stated she let the patient make this decision 'on his own.'"

Several weeks later, on March 25, Joe Willie woke up with long cuts and gashes on his left forearm. The sheets were soaked with blood. In his sleep he had torn at his skin and ripped through the flesh with his nails.

He looked at his sheets in terror and began to yell. "Mom! Mom! Come here!"

He was afraid to move. He didn't know what he'd done or whether it was serious.

"What is it?" She poked her head over the top of the stairs.

He didn't have to answer. "Joe Willie!" she cried when she saw the blood. She turned his arm over carefully and looked at the long wounds.

"Come on down and let me wash you up. You're just covered with blood."

Three days later it happened again. This time he'd torn around the bandages and cut at the skin that he'd left untouched before. He thought of vampires and monsters that attacked in the night and lived off the taste of human flesh.

It happened again and again and once he even woke up to find that he had tied one end of his long leather belt around his arm and the other end around the bed. He could barely move he was strapped so tight.

That day Mrs. Simpson drove Joe Willie back the forty miles to the hospital. This time he knew where he was going and he knew he was not coming back. They were quiet and they didn't say much in the car.

Later he apologized to the doctor for what he'd done. He said he was sorry and he didn't know how to explain it. "I've been tense," he said, and his answer was vague and unsubstantial.

"The patient," the doctor wrote, "was admitted to the usual male receiving ward."

"Because of his anxieties, apprehensions, and basic feelings of inferiority, he was started on Stelazine, five milligrams in the morning and ten milligrams at night."

"No one ever told us what was the matter with him," Mrs. Simpson remembered. "The only thing they ever said was he was going through puberty and hadn't decided whether to use it for good or bad."

Joe Willie was fifteen years old, and his sixteenth birthday was seven months off. He headed back inside where the walls were white, and pipes ran along the ceiling, and his bed was six feet from a guard. He stayed there four months this time and afterward he dropped out of school midway through the tenth grade. Later that winter he took the money he had earned cutting grass and cleaning windows and working in the drugstore and he rode out of town heading west. This time he didn't telephone back in the middle of the night and he didn't stop in the cornfields or the sheriff's office. He didn't return for a long time.

17

AS MANY AS EIGHTY people on the New York City payroll went to work Thursday on the case of Katherine Cleary. These included patrolmen, detectives, sergeants, lieutenants, one captain—Captain Ernest Fitzgerald, chief of the whole Fourth Division covering Central Manhattan —doctors, pathologists, chemists, clerks, and typists.

Their purpose, directly or indirectly, was to solve the murder but, even disregarding the fact that in this case there were no leads or clues, the chances of success were not terrific. There had been one thousand six hundred and ninety-one murders in New York City last year, and only fifty-six and one-half percent were solved. Nine hundred and fifty-five murderers were still walking around free and three hundred and thirty of these were in Manhattan alone.

The victim herself was naked, wrapped in a clean white sheet and stored on a movable tray in a long metal drawer. She was in the morgue, scheduled for an eleven A.M. autopsy. Her present temperature was about forty-two degrees Fahrenheit.

Five doctors participated in the autopsy. It lasted a good part of the day. The dissection was performed by the deputy chief medical examiner, three members of the staff assisted, and overall supervision was handled by the chief medical examiner himself.

The initial report on Case Number M73–88 was four pages long. It described the stab wounds in the neck and the stab wounds in the abdomen. It listed every bruise on the body, as well as the precise location, down to the quarter inch, and it analyzed the "wounds" inside the vagina. These, it found, were "superficial." It described the "trauma to the head and neck," and observed "the marked scoliosis" on the right back.

It was also discovered, for example, that there was a "fracture of the ninth left rib," the result, theoretically, of the murder episode, and noted, among other things, that the "small and large intestines are not remarkable," that the bladder was empty and the stomach contained only a few "particles of food."

There were, however, "OTHER TRAUMATA FOUND ON THE BODY." These, specifically, were bruises one and one-quarter inches in diameter above the left nipple. They were purple and "the rim of this area," it said, "shows indentations suggestive of tooth marks."

There was, further, "seminal fluid and spermatozoa" in the vagina.

On the last page the cause of death was typed in capital letters. "STAB WOUNDS OF NECK, ABDOMEN, INTERNAL JUGULAR VEINS, LEFT COMMON CAROTID ARTERY, LIVER AND STOMACH. HOMICIDAL."

THURSDAY MORNING there was a phone call at the 20th Precinct for "the cop working the murder."

Kraft took the call. "Which cop?" he asked.

"I don't know the name."

"What'd he look like?"

"Tall redheaded guy."

"We got a couple of those," Kraft said. "Cooley or McBride?"

"I don't know the name."

"Well, was he thin or a bit on the heavy side?"

"Real thin."

"That's Cooley. He's out. What's the message?"

"Tell him Rafe called. Tell him I got something for him and I'll be waiting to see him. At the Green Oaks Bar."

HOLYOKE HADN'T LASTED forever, and Katherine left the first chance she got. In 1962, after graduation from high school, she packed her books, her skirts, her kneesocks, and her jeans and went forty miles away to college near Newark.

Life in the white house had not been easy. People said Vincent and Mary quarreled like everybody does, about money and each other, and their children. It was like all families in the community. But what bothered Katherine, they said, was the set of rules they all believed their children had to follow. There, on the edge of Holyoke, as sure as the scent of lilacs in the spring and the wind in the fall, there was always "the right thing to do" and there was always its opposite. It was forbidden to lie or steal or hate. It was forbidden to do anything counter to some vague combination of Catholic and social doctrine.

And, someplace down the line, as the children grew older and learned to drive cars, the list of sins headed in a new direction. This was like a lot of Catholic households and in the beginning this sin wasn't even called sex, or premarital sex. It was just vaguely associated with the body and how to move it or clothe it. In due time, however, this began to mean how you touched it, or used it or felt it or loved it.

Later Mary Cleary was more explicit: Be careful, she warned Katherine. Sex can be a woman's downfall. Sex is bad, she said. Men are after only one thing. They'll take all you've got, but they only want to marry someone good like their mother.

But Holyoke didn't last forever. And leaving behind the yearbook that identified her as "kind," "fun," and "easy to get to know," Katherine enrolled at Newark State Teachers College. There her discontent found an identity of its own and she was among the first to enlist in the call for change that was developing in the country in the early sixties.

The civil rights movement was already in the coffee shops, and advisors in olive drab were on their way to that narrow strip of land on the other side of the world called Vietnam. There were stories in the newspapers about Alabama and Mississippi, Camelot and Cuba, but much of this drama escaped the people at Newark State. They were concerned instead with good grades, a good living, and security. They had grown up around the mills and factories of northern New Jersey where their parents worked and they believed in labor unions, low taxes, and the status quo. They had not applied to Yale, Chicago, or Berkeley, and their vision was satisfied by the state of New Jersey.

But Katherine was different.

She read the *New York Times* every day and she spent her spare time working in the headquarters of a local civil

rights organization. She dated black men who were study-
ing to be engineers and she loved the folk music that was
only then beginning to be popular. She bought posters for
her room and read omnivorously from the classics, philos-
ophy, psychology, novels, and magazines. She was already
preparing to be a specialist in the education of the deaf,
and she had a profound belief that all people were equal.

One of her close friends was a woman named Mary
McGuire. Mary now has a husband and a child and a
career and she remembers Katherine this way: "She was
much brighter than most of the people in the school. The
average woman who went to Newark State was lower middle class, not too bright, not stupid, mind you, but they
were placid, wore stacked heels and pantyhose, and used
hair spray. They were not bad people but I wasn't in that
crowd and neither was Katherine. We were the ones who
were involved outside and a lot more sophisticated, and
Katherine, even more than I, had her head in the real
world. She was curious, alert. That didn't come from her
family. It came from her."

Katherine and Mary met for the first time soon after
school started. It was the beginning of a friendship that
lasted for eight, even nine years. It was after dinner and
Mary McGuire was brushing her teeth at one of the sinks
in the large bathroom in the women's dormitory when a
short little redhead came in with her arms full of magazines.

"What on earth are you doing?" Mary asked. "Opening
a library?"

The redhead looked surprised—as if everyone took that
many magazines to the bathroom. "No," she said, "I'm

going to take a bath." Then she looked down at the pile
of *Harper's, Atlantic, Life, Newsweek,* and others in her arms
and seemed embarrassed.

"I think it's great," Mary said reassuringly. "I'll even
borrow them."

Mary McGuire grew up not far from Holyoke in a large
town by the water, called Passaic. Like Katherine she was
Irish Catholic and had been tagged for marriage and
domesticity since the days before she even went to school.
Passaic was a place of mills and factories and industrial
smog, and Mary felt as if she was locked up inside a me-
chanic's drawer. She hated it. She had to get away. And
for her, Newark State was a way to reach out for herself
somewhere beyond the hinterland of what she knew and
she recognized the same need and intensity in Katherine
Cleary.

Mary McGuire did not hear about the murder, or even
the death, of Katherine Cleary until years afterward. She
said she felt no dilemma about talking about her friend
because the way she saw it, to share her impressions would
ennoble Katherine and lend her life dignity, instead of
oblivion.

"Everyone liked her," Mary said one day. "She had a
terrific sense of humor and was down to earth. She had no
phony pretenses. Also, she was very generous. No matter
how much she had, if you needed it, she'd share with you.
If you needed fifty cents or a hair dryer or some extra
curlers or a blue bag to go with a blue dress, Katherine
would go down to her room and come back with something to give you."

Katherine was also ingenious. Among other things, she

devised a method for cooking without a stove. There were no kitchen facilities in the dormitory but she showed the others how to make a grilled cheese sandwich by wrapping the sandwich in tin foil and then cooking it by laying a hot iron on top of it. Another method involved taping the sandwich to the side of a hot clothes dryer the college maintained in the basement.

Mary McGuire talked for a long time.

"Katherine had thick red hair and lovely skin," she said. "A man would certainly find her attractive. But her whole experience as a child made her bitter. The surgery left a mark on her," she added. "At night when we were sitting around in the dorm or in the cafeteria, sometimes she would talk about it. And that was always special because you knew she liked you enough to confide in you. We weren't perceptive enough at that age to really understand what she was feeling or know how badly her self-esteem had been hurt, but we listened and tried to comfort her. She thought something rotten had happened to her," Mary went on, "and she thought she was screwed for life. There was a lot of hate and anger in her and a lot of it was directed at herself. Katherine concealed this bitterness, however, and especially in any kind of social or public situation, she concentrated on being funny and quick, almost showing off. She wanted to get attention, make friends. She made a joke out of everything. If you said to her, 'What do you think of Richard Nixon?', she'd say, 'Listen, be kind to him. He came from a mixed marriage. One of his parents was human.' She called our food in the cafeteria 'monkey food.' Once when the cafeteria woman was stirring a stew or something, Katherine quoted this long thing by Shakespeare, 'Double, bubble, boil and trouble, eye of goat, belly of lizard.' She made everyone laugh.

"Her favorite thing, though," Mary continued, "was what she called her 'High-C' joke. If she was in a bar or with a group of people, she would stand up like a comedienne and say: 'Now, for all my friends in San Diego, I'm going to sing high C.' And then she'd go, 'High C' [and Mary McGuire belted out Katherine's 'High C,' not in a high voice, but in a deep, deep baritone].

"She used to do her 'High-C' routine a lot. I remember sitting in the cafeteria all the time, and whenever there was somebody we didn't know, she would say, 'Oh, it's so tough being a music major. I had to practice and practice all day until I could hit high C. Want to hear me hit high C?' And of course everyone would say, 'Sure.' So she'd go, 'High C,' in that deep voice. It really cracked people up. It wasn't weird, it was funny. But she rarely got close with people. The humor drew people to her, but it also kept them away. Over all, I think it was a positive thing—but she did get too loud sometimes, too abrasive.

"Her best friend had no other friend besides Katherine and she never talked to anyone. She was always alone and the only person I ever saw her talk to was Katherine. When they were together, Katherine was a different person. She was always serious. Her friend had probably never even heard her 'High-C' joke.

"Her family was quiet too, and traditional—the don't-make-waves type, don't-get-involved, do-like-us. Katherine had broken out of that mold to a large extent. She was not religious anymore and she often talked about resenting the repressive aspects of Catholicism.

"I didn't get along with my family. The majority of

people at that school were plodding along in their own little ruts but the people Katherine and I associated with were independent, breaking away from their families, being themselves and no longer being protected by momma and poppa.

"Katherine and I in particular in the group resented the way girls were treated at home," Mary said. "I know I used to bitch about the fact that every time I went home on weekends I had to spend all the time cleaning the house while my brother never lifted a finger. It was the same at Katherine's. That's just the way it was then: brothers didn't wash floors and girls did. Katherine would tell us sometimes about how she had gone home for the weekend, really tired from school, and her mother would come into her room and say, 'Katherine, get out of bed. There's dishes to wash and work to do.'

"She didn't like that attitude toward girls, but she liked her parents a lot. The operation, though, had made her bitter. I think she was fighting off the idea that she deserved to be crippled. A lot went on inside Katherine. That's what attracted me to her. She was always thinking. Thinking about men. The state of the world. Where she was going to fit into it. What she was going to do with her life. Katherine asked big questions—the kind there are no answers to, but she had enough as a person to know these things existed, whereas a lot of people don't.

"Her involvement in civil rights was like that. It came from a moral and spiritual belief that these were God's children and they were the same as she. One time she and a group of friends, including at least one black guy she was dating, went to a diner in Newark. New Jersey is above the

Mason-Dixon line, but in those days it was still a very racist state. And when they sat down to be served, no one would serve them because there were blacks and whites together. But Katherine made them sit it out. They sat there and they sat there and they sat there. And I remember Katherine saying, 'I would have sat there until hell froze over.' And she would have.

"Finally the waitress came over to serve them and she asked Katherine her order and Katherine said: 'Coffee. Black.'

"But probably the main thing about Katherine, underneath it all, was her back. How can a woman have a deformed body—even slightly—and not have it bother her? I know she thought she was a disappointment to her parents. Look at the problems women have who have radical mastectomies. Some of them want to commit suicide and some of them do. Some of them won't have surgery, and choose to die instead. Katherine was bothered the same way. She had a terrific sense of shame about her body. After all, we all knew we had to get married someday. Katherine too. But I think she could have married."

KATHERINE GRADUATED from college with average grades in 1966. Afterward she moved to New York City and went to work as an elementary school teacher in the public schools of Newark, New Jersey. She stayed there for three years, during the period of time the city was torn by riots and chaos. Newark was the first northern ghetto city to be hit with urban strife and, although a number of other white teachers left, Katherine viewed it as a matter of political principle to continue working there.

Little is known about her first few years in New York City except that she lived in the relatively safe residential section of Manhattan known as the East Side, made a lot of friends, and probably had a more active social life than most single women who arrive without friends or relatives to live in the big city.

She lived most of the time with two roommates in a second-floor walkup in the East Seventies, and as a group they gravitated toward the style of life that is so common among some single people in New York. Later this became the most important feature of Katherine's life.

They hung out at night in bars.

They didn't go to the big expensive places that were famous "singles" joints full of out-of-towners on the make. Nor did they go to the sleazy spots where free sex was as available as peanuts. Their style was very different. They went to the neighborhood bars, the places where men watched football on weekends and women could stop by for hamburgers or a drink without being accosted by rudeness and male assumptions. These were the kind of places where all they had to do was make it clear they weren't in a hurry to reach the bedroom, and then the situation was as casual as someone's living room.

Katherine, for her part, understood that New York could be the loneliest place in the world and she told people she wanted to be "fun to be around." She tended to be quiet during the week, but to "live it up," as she put it, on weekends. This meant, in her case, she even got drunk and had to be carried home and put to bed by her roommates. Her normal routine, however, was circumspect. She dated a number of people three or four times and knew others who invited her out once or twice a month. She apparently, however, had no long-term relationships.

During this period of time Katherine made at least one very important friend, a bartender at the Brown Jug, a bar on Second Avenue near her home.

He was several years older than she and handsome, with dark eyes and curly brown hair, and from the beginning it was clear he wasn't attracted to her or she to him. Perhaps that helped their friendship. His name was Steve Levine and he had grown up on the East Side of Manhattan, gone to private schools, but then reneged on family expectations of a career and drifted into the business of running a bar. He liked it. It was casual work and took advantage of his good nature and his instinct for people. He was planning to buy a bar of his own in the future. In the beginning the redhead named Katherine Cleary was just one of dozens of females he knew by sight, but then gradually, when she'd drop by and he'd say, "How you doing?," she wouldn't just say, "Oh, fine," she'd tell him.

In time she came to him regularly for advice, specifically about how to behave socially, to relate to men or get someone to like her. Katherine rarely articulated her anxieties, but she did reveal them, and Steve's problem with her was that she couldn't handle advice. She asked for it but then ignored it.

Once, for example, he tried to talk to her about being

loud and boisterous. His point was to get her to realize she tended to dominate conversations and should, he thought, try to be more mellow, less frenetic. Instead she only heard it as criticism. He wished he hadn't said anything because she got depressed, even defeated.

Another time she was talking about how difficult it was for her to deal with men. Steve figured she meant she was unhappy about not having any good relationships. He encouraged her, spoke about how intelligent she was, earnest and good, and in time, he said, a good man would know that and love her.

He suggested she try being less aggressive, try to be softer, sexier.

"But what if I'm interested and they're not?"

"Well, that's not going to go anywhere."

"No, that's not what I mean," she said. "What if there's somebody I like and he doesn't even notice me?"

"Just be subtle, that's all."

"Subtle," she repeated quietly, as if not sure how that applied to her. And then, he said, she got up and went home. She was depressed. He came to realize even back then, he said, that she didn't know how to behave in the world. She didn't know which, if any, of her masks and costumes were real. She was, he said, "a very troubled lady." She'd come in one day, for example, and talk about how depressed she was, how terrible she was as a person. The next day she'd be on top of the world and chatter on, as if totally unaware of the person she'd been yesterday. And then the next day, perhaps, she'd be angry at someone, or irritated, or just in a bad mood.

But the point was, he said, she seldom recalled her

previous behavior. It was as if she was no continuous person, just a package of costumes that changed.

Sometimes he didn't know how to deal with her, he said, and got annoyed. He thought she used him, simply toyed with him to satisfy her own moods, and it came as no surprise, he said, that she was unable to develop any serious relationships. "She didn't know how to be intimate," he said. "She didn't even really know how to be interested in someone else."

Generally, though, he said, he understood what she was going through and felt generous toward her, and supportive. As the years passed, Katherine grew to trust him more and more and he too became very fond of her and adopted the stance of a protective older brother.

ONE NIGHT SOMETIME in 1967, when Katherine was twenty-five years old, she was sitting at the Brown Jug with some friends.

"How you doing, Katherine?" Steve asked.

"Fine."

"Oh, come on, don't be down. Life's not so bad," he retorted.

The evening wore on and by eleven thirty the bar was almost empty. The jukebox was turned off and Steve himself was sitting on a stool reading. It was a slow night.

Somebody was watching a movie on the television and outside it was raining.

A middle-aged man, who'd been drinking Scotch all night alone, moved down the bar away from Steve to take the empty stool next to Katherine. Steve didn't pay him much attention, but looking up he noticed a lot of Katherine's leg there.

"Hey," the man said drunkenly to him. "I want another."

Steve came around the bar and poured him a drink. The man was heavily wrinkled. He had gray hair that was thinning on top and he smelled of alcohol.

A few moments later Katherine suddenly shrieked.

The man had taken out his penis and was rubbing it, soft and limp, against her leg. Holding the pink flesh in his hand, he was moving it up and down along her pantyhose.

"You goddamn son of a bitch!" she yelled full blast.

The man cowered back but Katherine reached out with her arm and slapped him across the face. The sound echoed in the empty room.

The man flung his hands up to protect his head. His penis was still dangling outside his pants. Katherine threw her drink at him. "You creep," she screamed, as the liquid streamed down his face. "What do you think you're doing?"

"Come on, fella," Steve said, as he took hold of the man's arm. "Let's go."

Isabel, a friend, tried to catch Katherine's arm, but she was in hysterics. "Get him out of here," she yelled, "get him out of here."

"Calm down," Isabel said. "Calm down."

The man was whimpering like a dog and paralyzed, unable to move. Katherine reached out and slapped him hard, once, twice, across the face. Then the man started to cry and suddenly he ran out of the bar with his hands over his face, his overcoat dragging on the floor behind him.

"My God, Katherine, what happened to you?" said Isabel.

"Take it easy, folks," Steve said to the other customers. "It's all over." Then he poured a Scotch and handed it to Katherine.

She was standing very straight. Her head was arched high and she shook it as if trying to shake dust from her hair. For a moment she looked triumphant and powerful, like a victorious queen facing herself in the mirror.

Then she took the glass and swallowed the liquid at one gulp. "Fucking creep," she said contemptuously. "He couldn't even get it up."

"You sure do have a temper," Steve said.

"Didn't you know that before?" she asked coyly but proudly.

"I suspected," he said sarcastically. "But, honey, next time something like that happens, just ask me to come over and handle things. That's what I'm paid for."

"He took me by surprise," Katherine said, suddenly on the defensive. "I'm never at my best when I'm surprised."

"You were lucky that time," Steve said. "He could have turned on you."

"Don't worry. I just didn't have my wits about me. It wasn't anything."

"Katherine, honey, the guy was pathetic. Don't you feel sorry for him?"

"Sorry for him?" she said angrily. "He's a bum and he deserves everything he gets. I just wish I'd gotten him in the balls."

"I NEVER KNEW MUCH about Katherine's personal life after she moved to New York," Mary McGuire said. "I was living in New Jersey. But we were both teaching in Newark in the public schools. We used to meet for coffee or lunch.

"We talked about the good old days, but we didn't have as much to share as before. I didn't feel very close to her anymore. I thought she was showing me a front but I couldn't get behind it. She always said she was fine and she made a point of saying she went out a lot and I guess it was true. We both missed college and the sense of community and security it provided. I thought she was sad.

"Mostly, though, we talked about work. Teaching in Newark was difficult. I only lasted a year. Others did it for two. Katherine made it for three. It was a terrifying experience for me. And when the riots started, it got even worse. People said it was dangerous and we shouldn't work there.

"It was easier for Katherine than for me. She had this immensely strong belief system, and what she was doing fit into that. I'd look into the faces of my students and see more misery and anger than I knew how to deal with. I think Katherine looked at them and identified with them. I kept trying to figure out what I wanted to do with my life and I didn't think I had to spend it that way in Newark. But Katherine didn't think like that and being in Newark meant a lot to her. I finally left, but she stayed another two years, until 1969, I think it was. Then she just gave up and left too."

The school clock said after five. It was 1969. Katherine was late going home. Usually she tried to make an earlier bus back to New York. The street sounds outside penetrated the silence of the old stone building, and Katherine looked down at the charts and lessons, papers and grades, spread out before her on the desk.

There is no way of knowing exactly what took place at the school that afternoon. Later Katherine only told friends bits and pieces, but it may have happened something like this:

At first she heard a noise. It sounded like the door behind her, opening. She turned around to look but the door was closed.

The clock was ticking and something made her wish she had already left.

She heard the door squeaking again and turned quickly, in time to see it shut. Someone was there after all. Then there was silence again.

A teacher she dated occasionally had told her to be careful. He said the situation in Newark was "volatile" and she should be "sensible." One of the things he said was "never be too alone." At three thirty, when she'd decided to work late, she'd remembered what he said. She wondered if she had been careless to stay late. That's what he always said. "Katherine, you're just too careless. You think something makes you immune from danger, and that's stupid."

A bus went by on the street outside, and Katherine straightened the desk, put the sheets back in the drawer. She could stay in the room and lock the door, or spend the night. Or wait until the janitor came. But there was nothing bad outside, she argued. Nothing was going to happen to her.

She stood up, swung her jacket over her arm, and crossed the room. The door squeaked as she opened it and she went out into the hall.

The long corridor was empty and she headed toward the stairs.

Suddenly a door behind her opened and a young black boy sprang at her. His fly was open and his penis was sticking out, thick and full. She tried to push him away, but he grappled with her little body and finally squeezed her around the neck with his arms.

There was a long pair of scissors in his right hand and he tickled the blade against her neck. "All right, Kathy," he said, his breath coming hard. "How you doing? How you like it?"

He pushed his groin against her fanny, quick and urgent, and she felt the penis, long and hard, jamming at her as if trying to break a hole in her skirt.

She struggled against his arms to get away and tried to shout, but he squeezed harder against her throat. "Stop

it, Kathy. You'll like it." His hand went inside her blouse
and it moved over her chest.

She felt her breasts tingle.

"I'm gonna fuck you and you'll like it."

"No," she moaned. "No."

"Give it to me, Kathy, open up. Let me in."

"No-o."

His voice was getting harder, angrier. "Come on." He
pulled her over toward the side of the corridor and tried
to jam her up against the wall. Then he started to drag her
down to the floor. "It's so hard I'm gonna shove it in you."
He was moaning, too, as his hands were under her skirt
and moving into the wetness in her body.

Then suddenly as he turned she twisted and slipped out
of his grasp. Screaming, she got to her feet and started to
run. He grabbed at her. He ripped at her blouse and tore
it off her back.

Crying and sobbing, she ran down the hall. Her back
and breasts were bare.

She reached the stairs and saw the boy behind her, no
more than twelve or thirteen years old, going through a
window at the back that led to the fire escape; then she ran
down the stairs to the janitor and safety—and New York.

But in the second when she looked at the boy as she
wrenched herself away from him, she had seen the expression of shock, even contempt, on his face, as his grasping
hand tore her blouse and exposed the scar and swelling
to his eyes.

To her as she headed toward her future in New York,
the look confirmed everything she had always assumed to
be true.

23

"I'VE BEEN WORKING on it real hard," Rafe said, "and I've pulled that night back in closer to my mind. I can see Katherine sitting in the corner and then I can see her up close next to my shoulder. And I can see two guys. Sitting next to me."

He looked at Cooley. "Those the ones you're interested in?"

Cooley nodded.

It was midafternoon Thursday in the Green Oaks Bar and he and Rafe were drinking coffee. So far the investigation into the murder of Katherine Cleary had turned up no leads. In the whole apartment, for example, there was only one unidentified print and even it was smudged.

"These two guys were definitely together?" Cooley asked.

"I didn't see them come in, but they was sure sitting there like they knew each other. This one guy, the older one, didn't drink but he bought himself drinks and then he slid them down the bar to the other."

"Which one's which?"

"There was two guys. One was older. The guy next to me, he had an accent, he was younger."

"Accent?"

"I don't know. Like out west. He didn't sound like a New Yorker."

"What'd he look like?"

"I can't remember. He said he was looking for a job. I asked him what he does and he said he does anything. Said he wanted an office job."

"What about the other guy?"

"He didn't say anything. Except he said he was going home, and then he went."

"Then what happened?"

"Nothing."

"Katherine came up?"

"She came up and she talked with this guy."

"Did they leave together?"

"I didn't see that."

"What else did he say?"

"He said his name was Charlie. I said mine was Rafe. He bought me a couple of drinks. I let him, he wants to, fine by me, but I didn't buy him one. He acted big, like he had a lot of cash. Said he was in town for a few days. Said he traveled a lot with his jobs."

"What else?"

"Nothing. He asked me what I does and I said little of this, little of that. Said I drew pictures of people. He didn't believe me. I showed him my pad, said I'd draw him one. He had so much money I figured, let him send it my way. I charged him six dollars. Never charge more'n three usually."

"What'd you draw?"

"He didn't ask me to draw him. He said, 'Draw me a picture of Mickey Mouse.' I did. And then he said, 'Draw me a picture of Donald Duck.' And I did."

It didn't take Cooley a second to know what he had now. Either Charlie Smith had been in apartment seven-one-five, or else he'd given Katherine the pictures and she'd taken them home. Either way, Charlie Smith was someone the police had to find.

They still hadn't been able to locate Freddie Watson. He wasn't at home.

THE BUS WAS HEADING west. Sixteen-year-old Joe Willie Simpson sat in the back, his blond hair falling over his eyes, his thick-muscled arm resting on the windowsill. Behind him somewhere was the house in Viola Camp and the long gray building where grown men and children were strapped to their beds.

He didn't know where he was going. He just knew he was going after his future. He felt bad leaving his mom and dad—he loved them a lot—but he knew he had to get away. Things had gone on long enough, and he had to be on his own. He never considered himself a runaway—he was a searcher.

It was a long journey. He went through California, New Mexico, Nevada, Arizona, and Colorado, and sometimes he bought tickets. Sometimes he hitched a ride. Each time he stopped off somewhere, it was the same; he took his duffel out of the belly of the bus, or lifted it off the back of the truck and said, "So long." Then he slung the khaki bundle over his shoulders and set out afoot. He looked good. His jeans were tight, his boots dusty, and his eyes moved straight ahead. He held his head high and acted like he could take care of himself.

Sometimes he did.

He learned where to panhandle and where to sleep at night, where to get jobs stirring up eggs and fries in places nobody asked his age or reason. They just looked him in the eye. There was something about him even then that said he was okay. It got him jobs, rides, buddies, and dope. He got real good at waiting on tables and doing short orders, but mostly he got real good at the kinds of things they didn't teach back in Viola Camp.

He learned how to spend his money fast, how to drink whiskey, and how to tell the good from the bad when a guy laid down a taste of grass or coke. He learned the parts of town that smelled the most, were open the latest, and had the cheapest rooms upstairs. He'd lie awake at night on sheets that hadn't been changed in weeks, and listen to the toilet flush down the hall. He knew these hotels weren't any place he planned to stay for long. They were just part of his trip somewhere else.

It went on like this, month after month. One day he was sitting in a diner outside Reno, Nevada. There was a man next to him with lines down the side of his face and dirt in his knuckles. He wore a broad brown hat with hair oil seeping through the felt, and his trousers were greased with the stain of animals and work.

"How you doing, boy?" the man asked.

Joe Willie looked over at him. "Fine," he said, smiling.

"You looked pretty deep in thought there for a while

and I was wondering to myself what a kid like you was doing out here by himself this early in the morning. You live around here?"

"No, sir, I don't," Joe Willie said. "I been hitchhiking."

"You run away from home?"

"Not exactly. My mom and dad know where I am. I'm looking for work and looking for a place my pop can buy. We're looking for a ranch, for the three of us and my little brothers and sisters. My dad's tired of city work. He's been working in an office all these years and he wants to put his savings in a piece of land. It was my idea," Joe Willie continued, as the man listened. "It was my suggestion. I been working on them for years to get out of the city and now my mom's gotten sick and they agree country life is what we need. A ranch and some cows."

"Sounds good," said the man.

"A ranch and some cows." Joe Willie could even picture it in his eyes. It was the first time he'd said it aloud. The dream had been coming for a long time, but now it was taking shape in words and ideas and he saw the stock of hay, the barn, the farmhouse.

"It might even be," he continued out loud, "that my pop would set me up. We don't actually know for sure my mom can move. She might have to stay near the doctors back home, but my father wants to set me up in something and I'd sure like to go into the ranching business. Right now I'm just looking for work on a ranch so's I can begin to know the business. A ranch and some cows, it'd be a good thing." It was as if the words lulled him into a peaceful spot where he wanted to linger and the conversation died out like a fire that finally sputters to an end, and the man and the boy were quiet.

After a while the man finished his breakfast. "You got a place you're headed for right now?" he asked.

"I just come from Winnemucca," Joe Willie said with a grin.

That was a windswept village in the middle of the north Nevada desert with an airstrip, a highway, and a lot of bars. Winnemucca was the lawful prostitution center of the western world and a whole lot of women there made a living lying flat on their backs for short stretches of time. Joe Willie himself had made several payments there and now he was broke. "Whyn't you go on up to Reno and make some money on the tables?" one woman had said to him. "You can't help win something."

"I'm headed for Reno, where I got an uncle owns a hotel," Joe Willie told the man.

"How'd you like Winnemucca?"

"Not bad. Not bad." He chuckled and looked at the man knowingly.

Actually the women had been okay but what he liked best about Winnemucca was the going in and the going out. He liked the outskirts of town where it was full of sand and dry hills and cows and it was in that place that Joe Willie had begun to feel the pullings of the silence and the rhythm.

He had stood there on the highway waiting for a car or truck to stop and the idea had begun to take hold in his mind. He sat down on the side of the road and leaned his head back into the sage. He could see the dust turning into green fields, the barren land a spot for sheds and a barn. Stars at night and coyotes yowling on the faraway hills. It would be good. It was as if the noise and cold stone walls in his head would be pushed back forever by the space and silence of the western desert.

"I'm thinking of telling my dad to come back up around here to buy a ranch," he told the man. "My uncle down in Reno's gonna have some good ideas and I think we'll fix it up."

But there was no uncle and nothing to fix up and months later Joe Willie ended up back in Viola Camp. He was home again. He was eighteen years old and it was 1968. There were cubes of acid in his duffel and leftover pieces of grass and stems in his pocket. He had reeked of alcohol and dope for a long long time and flashed on colors and scenes the flatlands of Illinois could never provide.

Back home it was quiet. His mom and dad were away at work and Fred and Sue Ann were at school. Far away in New York City Katherine Cleary was still teaching in Newark and living in New York. She went to movies, read books, dated a lot and told people she wanted to be independent. Her mother asked, "Aren't you frightened of New York, Katherine?" And her daughter said no.

Back in Viola Camp there was nothing to be frightened of. Joe Willie sat there in the living room five feet from the street and felt safe—as if the chintz and white bread, the mongrel dog and sounds from the kitchen allowed him to relax. It would be like that from now on: This house became his haven from the outside world.

He went to work at Pasquale's Pizza Parlor and rented a room for himself in town. Less than a year later, he left. It was springtime and in New York Katherine, now twenty-five, had quit her job in Newark and gone to teach at St. Joseph's School for the Deaf in the Bronx.

This time Joe Willie headed south and then east. He went to Texas, Georgia, and, finally, he reached Miami. He had already made plans. This time he intended to settle down. He enrolled in high school, slept on the beach, and kept his books in a locker in the bus station.

"Ma'am," he said to the school official, "my folks come here last month, but I didn't register for school right off like I should have because my daddy took off with another woman and left my mom high and dry. I had to help out at home and I been working every day to get us some money. Now I got that under control and I want to get back into school."

The woman was impressed. "Good for you, Joe Willie," she said.

And Joe Willie headed off again into the tenth grade. He did his math and English as he sat looking at the sunset on the beach, and he wrote his papers in the diner where the buses came in. He tried real hard to make it work, but it didn't happen. He dropped out of school and took to the streets full time.

Then after a while he took off again. This time he went to New York and Times Square. There he gravitated toward the bright lights and the little bars underneath. He felt at home here in this netherland of neon signs and cheap whiskey, of lost hopes and lost dreams. He made friends with men like himself who were picking up bits and pieces, living like scavengers, and he took to hustling and stealing and, as the night hours turned to morning, he learned to pick up lonely strangers of the male sex who were willing to pay for a few moments of pleasure.

Joe Willie had found a new way to earn a living, and he charged from twenty dollars to fifty dollars for a slow ride in an elevator up to a hotel room where the man who paid bent down on his knees in front of him and opened his mouth wide.

Joe Willie had first started to earn money this way in Miami but in New York he turned his handsome male body, strong legs, and ass into a lucrative way of life. He got into cars with strangers and he went to townhouses on the East Side. For his own pleasure he still preferred women, but he learned to readjust his charm in order to make a living. He had just the right measure of contempt and flair, and the men with the dollar bills kept coming. He began to make as much as three, sometimes four hundred, dollars a week and he kept it all in cash in a brown leather wallet next to his hip.

For the first time in his life he had plenty of money and he spent it fast. It was "dirty money," he said, and the longer it sat around unused, the more it soured.

ONE NIGHT IN JUNE 1970 Joe Willie was drinking in the Club Forty-six on 46th Street off Times Square. He was twenty years old. Katherine had moved into her own apartment on the Upper West Side on 87th Street, and Joe Willie had connected with friends from Miami. They were all living in hotels along the dark sides of the Great White Way. Between tricks, Joe Willie met them at the Club Forty-six, a topless bar, for drinks.

The place was unswept, unwashed, and it smelled. But to Joe Willie it was home. He felt at ease there, and as time went on the alley cats on the chairs, the glasses in the corner, and the red and blue light bulbs were the landmarks in a room of his own.

The women dancers moved above him on the top of the black formica bar; and he'd stand there in his faded jeans and boots and look up between their legs. Their breasts wobbled when they danced, and the short hairs curling out along the edges of their tiny pants twisted under the elastic. They liked Joe Willie and every now and then they leaned down over the bar and let him lick up between their legs or along the nipples of their breasts.

This hot night in June he had had no tricks, and had sat there for several hours drinking. It was after midnight and the place was almost empty. The dancer was kneeling on the bar talking to a customer, and Joe Willie had been staring at the formica for almost an hour. He was scratching his arm.

Finally the bartender interrupted him. She had known him for months. "Hey, cowboy," she said.

He looked up.

"Whatsa matter?" she said. "You trying to dig a hole in your arm? You don't look so good."

"Just thinking."

"About what?"

"Nothing much. I don't feel the greatest. You decide to quit yet, like I been telling you?"

"No."

"How long I been telling you? You're better 'an this. You went to school. You got an education."

"I know," she said, "but what about you?"

"What do you mean, what about me?"

"When you gonna get outa what you do?"

"What do you mean?"

"I know," she said. "I see everything. You think I don't know what's what? With the men and all?"

"This is just an on and off thing for me," Joe Willie said. "Temporary. I'm getting my life together and when I'm ready I'm gonna settle down and buy a ranch. Right now I'm making a lot of money."

"I bet you are. I can sure understand why, too."

Joe Willie shifted his eyes, embarrassed. Diane laughed. "Why, look at you. A compliment like that and you're blushing. Don't the ladies tell you nice things like that? Or just the men?"

"I don't care what they say," Joe Willie said. "It's easy and it's about the only thing I can do well."

Then he got up and left the bar.

He went outside into the air and crossed the street to the telephone booth on the corner of 46th and Broadway. He called one of his friends from Miami who was staying in a hotel nearby. "Hey, Phil," he said, "come on down and have a drink . . . I'll wait for you on the corner."

Joe Willie stood there waiting.

Then a man went by. Joe Willie looked at him and the man looked back. The man continued walking.

26

THE MAN WAS TALL and thin with reddish blond hair and black-rimmed glasses. He was thirty-nine years old and he came from a farm in Illinois, where his father owned a grain elevator and his mother raised her sons not to swing on trees or dig in the ground.

His name was Danny Murray and he looked at Joe Willie Simpson outside the phone booth. Their eyes caught for a second and Danny kept walking. It was "a magic moment," he told a friend afterward. "There was something incredibly powerful about him. I've thought about it a lot and tried to figure out what it was I saw in him the very first time I laid eyes on him. I don't know. It was strength."

He paused. "No," he said, "it was endurance."

Daniel P. Murray had come to New York City years ago, spurred on by the dreams of jobs and success a little town can nurture but never fulfill. Now he had paintings on his walls and a bank account in four, sometimes five, columns. He had a penthouse apartment with a view of the sky, a closet full of clothes, and the air of a man with cash in his pockets and friends to spend it with.

But this hot summer night he was walking a long way from home. He was dreaming and wondering and missing the kinds of things he thought money couldn't buy. He was down here in Times Square to buy the very thing he knew money could buy. It was male and young and poor and it came out on the street and stood in doorways. Once off the street it pocketed a handful of dollar bills and crawled down easy between the sheets. There, very nicely and simply, it took care of the kind of thing Danny needed regularly. Sometimes, when he needed it real bad and there was no one to turn to, then, every now and then, it wasn't enough to wait. He had to come and find it and buy it.

After Danny Murray saw the man on the corner by the phone booth he kept walking, but he couldn't forget the expression on his face. He forgot about the pickup he was after and thought, instead, about the man. "Had it been a smile? Or just a look of warmth?" he said afterward. "Had he nodded? Or only moved his head?"

He passed the cinema and the clothing store. At the next corner he turned left and went around the block. He passed Sixth Avenue and the restaurants and cheap hotels and came back down 46th Street toward Broadway and the phone booth.

The man was still there, talking to someone, but he noticed Danny coming.

Danny walked on purposefully. He didn't want to look lonely or available, or as if he was after a piece of merchandise. He wanted, instead, to be himself, or, if anything, he wanted to be courted.

Out of the corner of his eye he watched the man and this time, he said later, "There was a smile on his face. Almost a nod, like 'How are you? How you doing?'—the faintest look to encourage me. But I wasn't about to go up and say, 'Hello' or 'Got a light?' I couldn't have done that with that man."

He went off in another direction and did not intend to return. About half an hour later, however, he found himself headed back toward the same corner. "I was actually hoping he wouldn't be there," he said. "My fingers were almost crossed he'd be gone. I was afraid of something."

But the man and his friend were still there, talking. "When he saw me coming he looked a little surprised. He separated from the other guy, and as I walked by he said, 'How're you doing?' "

"I'm okay," Danny answered. "How are you?" He walked on very slowly.

"Okay. Sure is hot out tonight," Joe Willie said, walking a little, too.

His voice was strong, vibrant. It sent shivers up Danny's spine, and he was afraid his excitement would show. He wanted to seem aloof, cool.

"You don't have a light, do you?" Joe Willie asked.

"Actually, I do," Danny said, stopping. He put his hand in his pocket and glanced at the man's thighs. They were narrow and hard—the jeans tight. He handed Joe Willie his gold lighter.

Joe Willie took it. "My friend and I been standing here trying to figure out what to do on a hot night," he said, as he took a long pull on the cigarette.

"I guess, just try to keep cool."

"Everyone looks hotter than shit, 'cept for you," he said, looking at Danny.

"Why me?"

"You look so comfortable you should be up in the mountains. You must have some kind of magic formula. Me," he said lightly, "all I can do is keep walking so the breeze goes by. Hey, you wanna take a walk uptown with me?"

Danny didn't answer.

"My friend Phil was just about to turn in for the night and I said I felt like a walk. He said he didn't. Why don't you walk with me, and then I don't have to work on him. Okay?"

"Sure, I guess so," Danny agreed. "I'm heading in that direction myself."

"Hey, Phil," Joe Willie said. "I'm going to take off. You get some sleep now, you hear, and I'll talk to you in the morning."

The two men headed off into the bright lights of Broadway and as they walked slowly, easily, Joe Willie talked and Danny listened.

Joe Willie talked about how tattoos are made and he said juniper extract is used to make gin. He said he thought prostitution and marijuana should be legalized and that the laws should be changed to give teenagers the same rights as adults. He also pointed out the place called Broadway Billiards on 52nd Street and told Danny a story about the great Luther Lassiter.

Danny said he didn't know how to shoot pool.

"Is that a fact?" Joe Willie said. "Why, it's the easiest thing in the world. Why, I could teach you in a day."

"Is that right?" asked Danny. "I may have to take you up on that."

"You do that. I mean, pool is fun; it's good for you, too, and you got nice long arms. You'd be a natural."

"Really?"

"Sure. Believe me. Basically," he said, "it's a matter of confidence."

"I've got a friend with a pool table in his living room, but he's very competitive. I don't play with him."

"Of course not," Joe Willie said. "That's natural. You'd have to be good first. You need a place where you can make all the mistakes you want and then you'll catch on fast. I promise you. Why," he went on with a laugh, "I can just see you in a month or two showing up at this guy's and then cleaning out the house. Might even be worth putting some money on the game—"

"You think so?"

"Sure. Except a fellow like you probably doesn't need the money. Boy, would I love to see that, though," he said. "You'd be terrific. You're real coordinated, right?"

They kept on heading north, and after a while Joe Willie said he was tired of walking. "But, you know, I'm not sleepy yet." And Danny suggested coming to his place for a drink. Joe Willie said that was a good idea. Not much open this time of night.

They got a cab and Joe Willie sat there next to the man in the back seat. He watched him open his wallet to pay the fare. "Hey, I bet you're not from New York," he said in his round rolling open way.

"No. What about you? Where you from?"

"Me, I'm from everywhere."

The doorman greeted them, and not much later, upstairs on the thirty-second floor, where 69th Street nears the Hudson River where Katherine Cleary used to watch the ships go by, they made love.

All night long they rolled around in the double bed that looked out over the river and the New Jersey sky and by some time the next morning Daniel P. Murray was in love with a man he knew was a con artist and Joe Willie Simpson thought he was on to a good thing.

"I gave him my phone number," Danny said, "and hoped he would call. I was sure he would."

TWO DAYS LATER JOE Willie called to say he was going to play pool. "You wanna come?" When they parted the next morning, Joe Willie said he knew a Greek restaurant with "terrific" baklava.

"I bet you'd love it," he told Danny. "You want to go?"

"Sure."

They made plans for that night, too, and once again ended up late at the billiard hall on Broadway and went home together afterward.

In the morning they ate breakfast up the street in the coffee shop near Tweed's, and Joe Willie said, "You know something I haven't done in ages?"

"What?"

"Go to a movie."

"Well, why don't we go?" said Danny.

"You want to?" said Joe Willie, excited.

"Sure."

It went on like this. They met at night and parted in the morning, and Danny knew little about his newfound friend. Joe Willie told him he lived downtown and was unemployed. He said he had graduated from high school but he didn't say where. He said he had been drifting around ever since and he made it sound like a fine and adventurous thing. But Danny wondered. Sometimes Joe Willie mentioned having a job interview, but Danny suspected it was a lie, and he recognized that he really knew nothing about how Joe Willie spent his days. He looked at the young man, fifteen years his junior, and he didn't ask him any questions. He regarded Joe Willie's silence, and even Joe Willie's pretenses, as his prerogative and his choice. But he listened closely to the sounds in Joe Willie's voice and he saw the look in his eye and afterward nothing surprised him.

In truth, though, when Danny went down into the subway on the corner of Broadway and 72nd to go to work, Joe Willie stood alone on the sidewalk. Sometimes he stared after Danny and felt the tide of people flowing by as if he was a boulder blocking their path. Then he would turn and walk south down Broadway, toward the Times Square area a mile and a half away.

About midmorning he reached Times Square, and it always felt like coming back to safe territory. Sometimes he joined J. Philip Wallerstein in his second-floor hotel room with the broken window and the sheets that were never changed, and they smoked dope and passed the time. Phil usually had a woman with him, often just a teenager, and sometimes when he went out to get breakfast or the paper the girl stayed. Joe Willie then picked up where Phil had left off. He rarely found a woman for himself.

Sometime later in the day, Joe Willie moved off to his

own room and called men he had met. He lined up appointments in thirty- to sixty-minute time slots and made between fifty and a hundred and fifty dollars the rest of the afternoon.

He saw Danny two, four, or sometimes seven times a week and it went on like this for months. There were, however, periodic interruptions when Joe Willie suddenly disappeared. Then, after a week or two or three, he'd call again.

"Where have you been?" Danny asked.

"I had to go out of town," Joe Willie'd say.

Within several months, after the two men became friends, Joe Willie let Danny know about his actual line of work, but he still remained very secretive, almost incapable of divulging full or accurate information about himself. And so, in the beginning when he took off on trips, he'd say something vague, like, "Oh, I had to go visit a friend," or "Oh, I went to Atlantic City for the week."

After a while, though, he told Danny the truth. He said he needed to get away, "to escape." He felt things closing in on him, he said, and he needed a change. At first Danny wasn't sure what he meant, but then he realized that Joe Willie was responding instinctively, like an animal, to some kind of internal signal that triggered a need for a different environment, different pressures. And when these needs developed, he took off, he told Danny, for Miami or he went home to Viola Camp.

One day, Joe Willie looked up the name of Danny's company in the telephone book. He had never called him at work before. They had been friends now for more than six months.

"Hi," he said.

"How'd you get my number?"

"Phone book. I wanna go to the American Museum of Natural History. Up there where Teddy Roosevelt rides his iron horse. Any chance you can get off work this afternoon and go with me?"

"Why do you want to go there?" Danny asked, perplexed.

There was a long silence.

"Why do you want to go there?" he repeated.

"I don't know," Joe Willie said. His voice was quiet. "I like dinosaurs."

"You what?" asked Danny, amazed.

"I like dinosaurs."

"I never knew that," Danny said kindly.

"I think they're interesting. I used to be real interested in prehistoric creatures. I know a lot about them and I've been thinking, I haven't been to see them yet. I've never been to that museum. I know it means cutting work," he said, "but I thought you might like to come. I'd like to have you," he added.

Thirty minutes later they met at the feet of the iron horse.

That night Joe Willie told Danny he used to be on the museum's mailing list. He said he read the catalogues from cover to cover and put the pictures on his wall. He told him that once in school when he was ten he had a fight with the teacher because she wrote the word "terridactyle" on the blackboard and he told her she had spelled it wrong. She said she hadn't. He argued and she argued and then she punished him for it and made him stand in front of the class facing the jeering students.

After school he went to the dictionary to look up the

word. It wasn't there and he went to the books on prehistoric animals and found the *pterodactyl*. He had been right.

He told his mother and she said schoolteachers were "uppity." "They always think they're better 'an everybody else," she said.

Danny listened. He knew Joe Willie's feelings for him were changing, and his own heart ached. He wished he could spread his love and kindness back into the boy's history, and he told Joe Willie he liked to listen to him because he was interesting.

"You think so?" Joe Willie said excitedly.

Danny nodded.

Danny had a lot of friends, he knew the theater, and he liked good restaurants, but he recognized in Joe Willie traits of himself in a past childhood that wasn't as lost or hurt or unpromising as Joe Willie's. Joe Willie taught him to play pool and forced him to ride the merry-go-round in Central Park. He borrowed Danny's suits and learned to deal with headwaiters. He enchanted the older man with his charming, aggressive manner and, despite all, acted as innocence abloom.

But it didn't take Danny long to learn this was Joe Willie's front. He saw traces of the boy's insides everywhere, sensed the sadness and decay there, aloof and unshared, and it tantalized him. It made him want to help even more.

It was a while before Joe Willie told him about the long gray institution with the forty-eight beds to a room, or how it felt to be water whipped with a two-inch round stream of water beating at your stomach and see the uniformed man with the hose laughing. But, in the meantime, Danny sensed the truth. Joe Willie was the first person he had ever loved, and he saw in him the same signs of loneliness, wariness, and fear of betrayal that had once been parts of himself.

He hoped that with his help Joe Willie could overcome them.

The main thing, he figured, was to show Joe Willie he could trust him.

SOMETIME IN THE winter of 1970 or the early months of 1971, Joe Willie told the hotel desk clerk he was moving out. Phil Wallerstein, his friend, was with him at the time. Phil was going south in a few days because, he told Joe Willie, he was on to a good thing. A couple of guys were making a bundle tiptoeing through the unlocked doors of summer cottages down there and coming back out with television sets and watches. Now they were planning to expand their operation. It was a sure thing and anytime Joe Willie wanted in, Phil said, just give him a call. Joe Willie said he'd think about it, but that, actually, he was on to a good thing himself now and afterward he was going to get a job. Well, Phil said, if he wanted a change of scene or to take a breather before job hunting, the offer was open.

"I know you," Phil said. "Sometimes you just want out. You're like a guy caught in an elevator. You're screaming to get out."

Joe Willie was going to move into Danny's apartment.

Danny had encouraged him to forget work, forget hustling, and take a rest for a while. Then, when he felt good, he could set about job hunting. In the meantime, he said, it made more sense for Joe Willie to move in with him, temporarily. Since he ended up there all the time, he added, it was pointless for them both to pay rent.

Joe Willie agreed. "I can get my own apartment in a month or so when I'm ready to settle down and get a job." Danny had said lots of jobs were available for people without high school diplomas. He also explained that Joe Willie could always take the equivalency test and be eligible for better jobs.

Joe Willie packed all his belongings into five large suitcases and later that afternoon he took four of them to a storage company. There he put down a fifty-dollar deposit and set off with the remaining suitcase for the penthouse on West 69th Street.

"You sure do have a lot of things," Danny said with a laugh when he opened the door. Joe Willie's suitcase stood wider than his hips and it came above his knees.

"You think that's a lot," said Joe Willie proudly, coming in. "Why, I got four more bigger 'an this in storage."

"You always travel with that much?" Danny asked as he directed him toward a corner of the bedroom where he had put a new set of bureau drawers for Joe Willie.

"Of course." Joe Willie hoisted the case up on the bed and started to unzip it. "These are my things. I sure hated to put the rest in storage. I might need them anytime."

Danny sat on the bed and leaned back against the pillow to watch Joe Willie unpack.

The bureau had four drawers, and the one on top had

two dividers; and Joe Willie, it turned out, had a number of decisions to make about where to place his things and how to organize them into different categories.

It was, he said, the first time he'd ever had a bureau drawer.

Danny didn't say anything but that was what he'd figured when he bought the furniture.

Joe Willie had about ten pairs of jeans, at least twenty shirts, and a record album by Barbra Streisand called *Funny Girl.* He had a lot of old magazines, including one *Life* with a picture spread on the Midwest, and two *National Geographics* with layouts on the Polynesian Islands and rare sea creatures. Among his books was one by Jack London, a five-year-old almanac, and a manual on how to run a ranch. He also had two hard-core pornography books with pictures and large-sized lettering. "My father gave me these," he said proudly.

He had Band-Aids, aspirins, toothpaste, about ten belts, and cutout pictures of animals pasted on school paper. He had almost all the letters he'd ever received, including postcards from boys in school who'd gone away to summer camp and get-well cards from his mother when he was in the hospital. The bundle was about an inch thick and it was tied with brown string.

He also had an old dark red blanket that he carried with him everywhere, and somewhere between twenty and thirty pocket watches in various shades of metal.

Pocket watches, he said, were his favorite things.

The days passed and Joe Willie and Danny had a good time together. They laughed and talked and took a lot of walks, but neither one ever said anything about things like love. Instead they shared a lot of secrets. Danny told Joe Willie he used to like women and he told him about the three who had wanted to marry him. But, he said, that was all past now. It was years, he said, since he had wanted a woman for himself. What he wanted, instead, he said, was what women gave: a home and a family, of his own.

And Joe Willie told him about life in Viola Camp and the scratches on his arm. He told him about how his leg had gone cold and stiff and about how he'd wake up in the cornfields and about how he had lain in bed and seen the blood seep out of his arm and drip onto the sheets and had to wonder which part of him was trying to kill the other.

"You don't have to think about those things," he said, "but I do."

They had their own routine. They had cereal for breakfast at home and waffles up the street if they went out. When they met for lunch it was hamburger or pizza. At night they went to movies and restaurants, the theater and the pool hall, and during the day Joe Willie took walks by himself and went to double features.

At night they had a new sleeping arrangement. Joe Willie no longer went to the big double bed but slept instead on the couch in the living room. This began one evening when he said he was tired and needed a good night's sleep. "You don't mind if I sleep on the couch, do you?" and Danny said no.

Danny knew that Joe Willie hated being touched in bed at night when he was asleep. He also knew that Joe Willie had come to view sex with him as "a responsibility."

"He didn't dislike it," Danny told a friend, "but he only

did it for me. He knew how I felt about him and I think he thought he owed it to me out of obligation or fairness. And part of me did want him to feel obligated," he admitted, "because I did want him as often as possible. I wanted any connection with him I could get. I knew he could never really be tied down or 'bought' with money or bought with anything, but I wanted to be part of him any way that was possible."

And so it happened that Joe Willie slept alone on the couch except periodically late at night when he'd turn to Danny and say: "I'll tell you what. I'll let you sleep with me tonight."

That was his way of saying he'd join Danny in the double bed. It also meant they could have sex. Other times he would put it a different way. "I'll let you sleep with me tonight but on one condition. That you don't come over to my side of the bed." That meant, Danny knew, that Joe Willie didn't want to be alone.

That's the way it'd been between them for quite a long time, but now the weather was changing. Indian summer was over and twilight came early. The streets were dark and Joe Willie was getting restless.

Danny began to look in the classifieds on Sunday. He read aloud from the job offers and Joe Willie listened, but he didn't respond. All he said was, he had to think about it more.

He also mentioned several times that he had a friend in Miami named Phil Wallerstein. He could go into business with him, he said.

"What kind of business?" Danny asked.

"He repairs air conditioners."

Sometime in October, Joe Willie said he wished he had a motorcycle. He mentioned it casually one day when he met Danny downtown for lunch. "A motorcycle sure would be an easy way to get through traffic," he said.

Several days later, Joe Willie turned down the idea of joining Danny for lunch again. He said he didn't want to face the subways, and noted that if he had a bike it would be different. The whole idea of work, too, he said, would be better if he had a bike.

Joe Willie was drinking a lot, and instead of going out during the day, he stayed inside and watched television. His temper was irritable, and Danny knew he felt a lot of pressure about work. He suggested Joe Willie try the employment agencies, but Joe Willie said he didn't want to admit to some jerk he'd never finished high school.

One night Danny said, "You know what I think would be nice?"

"What?"

"A motorcycle."

"I agree," Joe Willie said sarcastically.

"Well, I'd like to get you one," Danny said. "I think it would make things easier."

"You're kidding," Joe Willie said slowly, almost cautiously. "It's expensive."

"I know. But I think you deserve it."

"I can't believe it," Joe Willie exclaimed. "Nobody ever did anything like that for me."

They agreed that on Friday Danny would cash a check for five hundred dollars and on Saturday the two of them would take the money and go shopping for a bike.

Friday night Danny brought the money home. He showed it to Joe Willie and they were both excited. They had sex together, slept in the same bed, and in the morning when Danny woke up, Joe Willie was gone. The apartment was empty.

There was no note on the icebox door or in the bathroom or on the table in the living room. Danny waited all day for a phone call, but it didn't come. He hadn't really expected it.

Joe Willie had taken his own suitcase, but instead of packing his own belongings, he took Danny's. He took his clothes, suits, shoes, socks, and shaving lotion. He took his watch, his pack of credit cards, and his brown leather wallet from Dunhill.

He also picked up the five one-hundred-dollar bills on the table and took them.

IT WAS 1970 AND Katherine Cleary was twenty-six years old. She moved into a small apartment of her own on West 87th Street. Her mother kept saying, "Katherine, aren't you afraid living in New York City?" And she kept saying, "No," and she wasn't. But there was something about her face and the wrinkles on her future that did frighten her.

This was a new world for her over here and she loved it. The grocery stores sold mustard greens and pigs' feet, refried beans and corn tamales, and the streets were barely lit at night. Garbage piled high in the gutters and the air was always noisy. Over here everyone was in the minority; black, white, Puerto Rican, woman and child, rich and poor, and it stimulated her. She identified with everyone. But it was also a sadder place than where she had lived before across town, and Katherine felt herself drawn into that sadness as if that too was a spot where she belonged.

She had left her life on the East Side behind and moved to a place that was not as safe or secure. Twice before she had done the same kind of thing, first when she went from Holyoke to college and later, after college, when, instead of returning to the safety of her home, she moved out farther into the unpredictability of life by settling in New York City.

Over here she faced not just the paradox of poverty mixed with wealth, the lucky with the unlucky, but the fact that everywhere there was something abandoned. Young, old, and in-between, everywhere she looked there were people alone and lonely, especially the old people. They sat like birds, by the hundreds in rows in the sun, looking and watching, but almost never talking.

This was a city of strangers and anonymity, New York was, and Katherine fitted in. She was as inconspicuous as the rest, and some part of her must have known it.

She had started working at St. Joseph's School for the Deaf. She taught underprivileged blacks and Puerto Ricans who were deaf and often did not know how to talk. Instead they made a series of distorted and misshapen sounds that Katherine had learned to translate, and sometimes she thought it was like talking to birds, sharing a secret language with wild birds, and she alone had the keys to their happiness. They were wonderful children, she told everybody who would listen, they were innocent, lovable, unscarred by life, but marred by their birth. It was so unfair, she said. Why them? Why her, for that matter? And she often felt that in helping them she was reaching out to find herself as well, as if her life belonged on the same area of ground as theirs.

The children must have sensed this belonging, too, because they loved Katherine. Children always did. They could see the kindness and warmth in her eyes and in her touch and read it in her voice; she was open and loving with them. It was always "Katherine this" and "Katherine that" and sometimes when she got back on the subway at night to come home to the West Side she wondered if she had left herself behind. Elsewhere, out of their sight, she felt misshapen and out of place, as if the oddity of her breed truly did not belong.

But no matter how much she loved her work, Katherine didn't let her life get swallowed up in the identity of that career. She knew about the spinster-teacher syndrome and she herself wanted as much contact as possible. Consequently, over on the West Side she gradually created the same kind of night life she'd had on the East Side, one that centered around the activity of the neighborhood bars.

For the first time now she was living without roommates and all her time was her own. Sixteen blocks to the south, Joe Willie Simpson had moved in with Danny Murray, and around the corner from Danny's apartment, Tweed's Bar on 72nd Street had been taken over by Steve Levine. He had finally bought his own place.

During the next few years Katherine would read Camus,

go to Off-Broadway plays, take night courses in psychology at Hunter College, and outline a plan to earn higher teaching credentials for her career. She dated young lawyers and knew artists who lived in the Village. She praised John Lindsay, admired Bella Abzug, and talked about women's rights and political reform.

The years were promising. She was coming into her own. Holyoke was a long way behind. She grew her hair long and liked the feel of all its redness spilling across her shoulders. Her jeans faded from use and she bought a hash pipe. She smoked grass and was even thought to use cocaine.

"She was a very lonely lady," said one man who sat with her in the shadows of the bars week after week. "But she had found a groove, a life-style. She had broken through her family's barrier and she was a visionary, in a sense, out on her own."

But still Katherine was like a lot of women. Some part of her was trapped. Much as she fought it, she believed her life would not be in order until it had a wedding and a dining room table, and she thought her loneliness at night was proof she was losing her grasp on her future. She saw the years stretching out there empty in front of her, and without even thinking about it, the goal she had set for herself was social success and male approval.

When she lived on West 87th Street there was probably at least one young man with brown hair and brown eyes and white hands who meandered casually through her life, and their relationship was like a lot of the encounters people said Katherine had.

There was one, for example, and his name could have

been Philip and he could have been a schoolteacher, too. They met at a friend's house once when Katherine went for pizza and Philip was sitting on the floor by the bookshelves, talking to someone else. He did not notice her and they were not introduced, but Katherine thought he was attractive and interesting, if a little surly.

Several weeks later the telephone rang on West 87th Street and it was Philip. "I didn't have anything better to do tonight," he said, "and I thought I'd give you a call . . . see if you wanted to get a drink or something."

"Sure," she said.

He asked her where she lived and said he'd meet her on the street in an hour. An hour later Katherine went out to the sidewalk and forty-five minutes later Philip arrived. They started walking south. He didn't say why he was late and Katherine didn't ask. They talked about their friends and Katherine told him about her students. She was having a good time; to her way of thinking, Philip was an interesting, complicated person.

Several hours later he walked her home, said good night, and left. Katherine wondered if he would call again and she stayed home the next few nights hoping to hear from him.

About a week later he telephoned and asked if she wanted to go to a movie. She did and that night, again, he didn't say much. She had to prove she was interesting and worthwhile, she told a friend. She viewed it as her responsibility to convince him he wouldn't be disappointed in her.

After a while Katherine and Philip began to sleep together and he even spent the night with her from time to

time, and it was sex as it usually was for her. She didn't
really enjoy sex, people said, and rarely had orgasms,
although she knew how to pretend she did. Katherine's
attitude, apparently, was that she should make a man feel
good about himself sexually and that that was the way to
prove herself to him.

Steve Levine had met Philip with Katherine several
times and one night she asked him what he thought of
Philip. She asked him about all her boyfriends. Steve said
he was okay.

"What do you mean 'okay'?"

"I don't know. What can I say? I don't know the guy. He
doesn't say much."

"He's a very quiet person," Katherine declared.

"I guess I'd find that boring."

"Oh, no. He's serious, intense."

Steve shrugged. "You've got different tastes than I do,"
he went on. "I like women who flirt and like to be sexy and
aren't afraid to come after me if they're interested. I bet
this guy doesn't even know you like him."

"I see him about once a week or so."

"But I bet you haven't talked about it. I bet you haven't
been open with him."

"I can't just tell him I'm interested or that I wish he'd
stop dangling me on a hook."

"Why not?" Steve said. "Why can't you just say, 'Look,
why are you messing around with me and my time? Are
you interested in me or not, and if you are, I want you to
start being nice to me.'"

"I can't say that," Katherine exclaimed. "I could never
say that."

"I know. But why don't you think about it, honey? It's a different way of looking at things. You don't always have to be on the bottom, you know."

"Oh, Steve, I'm trying. I'm trying so hard."

"I know, honey, and you're doing great work." After a while Steve went off into another part of the bar and Katherine sat there alone in the shadows.

There were a lot of people in Tweed's. She looked around for a minute and then pulled a book out of her handbag and laid it open on the counter next to her wine. She leaned forward as if reading, and her finger was even on the page, but she was listening to the sounds and the music, wondering if someone would disengage himself from that place of noise and latch on to her instead. She felt the shiftings and the movement in the room and sensed her own stillness and isolation there in the midst of it.

Across the room a young woman named Linda Finlay was watching her. She saw the red hair falling across Katherine's forehead, the baggy orange blouse covering her crooked back, and she wanted to reach out and push the hair off her face, make her sit up straight and proud. "Something about her made me want to cry," the woman said later. "She could be the most alone-looking person I ever saw."

Linda worked in an art gallery and wore skirts with high boots or tight-fitting jeans with sweaters and dangling earrings. She knew how to hold her head and put a touch of gray above her eyes, and after a while she went over to talk to Katherine. "Hi," she said. "How're you tonight?"

Katherine said something back, but Linda could see a

look of retreat and fear come over Katherine's eyes, almost like a new set of windows being put in place.

"I saw you sitting over here by yourself and thought I'd come over to talk," she told her.

But Katherine didn't want to talk and after a while Linda moved away and Katherine turned back to the page as if the straight lines there would hold her in place. She stared and stared and her eyes blurred on the lettering and lost their focus. The words turned into a fuzzy haze and in the background she heard the sounds and the voices, the rolling tones of too much alcohol and hostility and tension, and the little woman from Holyoke knew she was a long way from home.

The more she listened and waited, whether for herself or for someone else or for the coming of time, the more she was pulled back to those hours and days, years ago, when she lay flat on her back. She was waiting then, too. There were sounds in the living room, sounds from the kitchen, and from upstairs, from the road outside and the lawn in the back. There were sounds overheard, near and far away, sounds small, sounds large, and ever since then the presence of sounds themselves made her feel unconnected, invisible, and remote. Oh, where's Katherine? Katherine's far away, far, far away. You can't even see Katherine.

It could happen in a subway or in a room, or even in a movie. Some part of her would drift away from being in the middle of the sounds, to being alone, like a rowboat or a dinghy that is set adrift and ends up floating miles away on the currents of the water. And she would feel a vast chasm separating her from life and hope and a future, and wonder why she of all the people she knew had been marked with the ugliness, doubt, and memories. Why was she chosen for this?

She got up to go home. It was late and she was tired. She pushed her way through the crowded room and looked for faces to smile and say good night, but they didn't. Nobody watched her leave or saw her passing.

She walked up from Tweed's to Broadway, went down into the deserted subway, and took the train to 86th Street. From there she walked home alone past the garbage cans and the brownstones. She didn't look up. Her head hung low and she watched the cracks in the sidewalk as they passed beneath her.

It looked to her as if the cracks were widening.

TIME PASSED AND life didn't change very much for Katherine Cleary. She signed up for more special-education courses at Hunter College and dated more men. She continued to take the forty-five-minute subway ride up to the Bronx every morning to work and to divide her time at night between friends and the loneliness and bars. She wished she lived closer to 72nd Street, and along the way she must have realized occasionally that the separation between different parts of her life was getting wider and wider. The person who worked at St. Joseph's and loved the children was not the same woman who took books to bars, and the woman who couldn't fall asleep at night was not the same person who chattered at parties.

She had read about Catholics and women and their struggle to be free, but she couldn't give the struggle in her soul a name. She was doing guerrilla warfare with an enemy she couldn't find. Camus had written in one of his notebooks that the city is a place for people to retreat from other people. She found the passage and it seemed a warning to tear herself away from isolation before she was lost. She could hear him say it, cold, male, authoritative: "As a remedy to life in society, I would suggest living in the big city. Nowadays it is the only desert within our means."

IN 1972 KATHERINE moved farther down into the desert. The place she took was an empty apartment next door to Linda Finlay at Two-Five-Three West 72nd Street. She told her parents it was safer than most places on the West Side because it was, at least, on a big main thoroughfare. In Holyoke the Cleary children were all grown up. Both parents were free to work now and at night, as they all sat around the dinner table, the parents felt great satisfaction. Their children were heading off on their own. But still, from time to time, Mrs. Cleary worried about her eldest, away in New York, so much on her own. But, as she put it, "You have to trust them sometime. You have to let them be themselves."

Back in New York that's what was happening, and one night, May 6, 1972, Katherine Cleary took a big step toward being something that looked like herself.

The night started with no indication of what would follow, and what did follow took place with no indication of what, if anything, had made it happen. Some said Katherine was to blame: She should have known better. Others said, no, she was a victim and it was Freddie's fault. Freddie was a thirty-two-year-old unemployed black photographer. He was sitting alone in Tweed's that night. So was Katherine.

Either way, what happened did have a lot to do with Freddie Watson.

Freddie is five feet ten inches tall. He was known as a dangerous man with a violent temper and an overwhelming fascination with guns. He had a bad reputation up and down 72nd, and more than one person had seen him start a fight. He was "sick and twisted," people said. "The kind of guy you know you gotta watch out for." By the time May 6, 1972, happened, Freddie had been in Tweed's many times. He knew Steve; he knew the bartenders and he knew the people who hung out there. He had seen, if not talked to, Katherine Cleary a number of times.

On May 6, 1972, he got to know her better.

Katherine was sitting alone at the bar. Jack Pawling, the bartender that night, remembered afterward that she looked poorly. He asked what she wanted to drink; usually she just had wine. But tonight she said, "Johnny Walker Red."

Freddie Watson was at the bar, too. It was a slow night

and Jack wasn't very busy, nor, it appeared, was Freddie. He was full of nervous energy and he spread his restlessness out over the room, and Katherine, for her part, was near enough to catch it.

She was leaning on her elbows, tracing the cigarette burns on the bar with her fingers. She didn't have a book. She was just drinking and thinking.

"Hey," Freddie suddenly called down to her. "Whatsa matter with you tonight?"

Katherine ignored him. She didn't look up or even react. She just went on tracing the burns on the bar.

"Hey. Aren't I good enough for you?" Freddie sneered down at her.

Katherine shot him a look that must have landed somewhere in the middle of his chest, and her face was angry.

"Don't give me that," Freddie retorted.

Katherine went on staring at him contemptuously. Freddie turned away as if intimidated by her look.

But then, after a pause, he looked back. "Hey, come on," he said in a taunting way. "None of that, lady."

Katherine didn't say anything; she watched quietly as Freddie picked up his drink and moved down the bar to her side.

"Come on," he said. "I'll buy you a drink. Maybe we can make friends."

Katherine stared at him for a while, as if the idea was disagreeable, but then she said, "Okay."

They talked and after a while Katherine laughed. Maybe she was feeling better or maybe she had no doubts who was the better of the two.

Sometime later Katherine left the bar. A few minutes

afterward Freddie got up, too. Pawling watched as he followed her across the street and went into her building.

Several hours later the seventh-floor hallway at Two-Five-Three West 72nd was quiet. It was midnight and inside the apartment at the end of the corridor Linda Finlay was watching television with her boyfriend, Charlie. Suddenly, through the paper-thin walls, they heard yells and screams coming from Katherine Cleary's apartment next door.

"It sounds like someone really getting it," Linda cried, and she and Charlie rushed into the hall.

There they saw a man run out of Katherine's room. It was Freddie. Still half undressed, he was yelling and pulling on his clothes as he went. "You motherfucker!" he screamed, and then they saw him disappear down the stairway.

Katherine's door was open and Linda rushed in.

"You all right?" she asked.

Katherine was standing near the bed crying, holding her face in her hands. She was bruised and beaten, Linda said later, and she had a black eye and welts on her shoulders.

The room was a mess, and, stepping over a chair, Linda went up to Katherine and took her little body in her arms. "Are you all right?" she repeated.

Katherine nodded slightly. She was sobbing silently and Linda rubbed her head with her hands.

"What on earth possessed you to bring him up?" Linda asked.

Katherine shook her head and said nothing.

"He's the worst type. Why did you pick him?"

"I don't know," Katherine cried. "I don't know."

"You shouldn't be with someone like that."

"I know."

"You should know better. He's no good. He's the worst kind." The kind, she said, "who lives in a hotel and walks around with a bottle in a paper bag."

"I know," Katherine said.

"You ever do this before?"

Katherine shook her head and she shuddered, frightened.

"Don't worry," Linda said. "It's all over and now, at least, you'll know better."

That was Saturday. The next day Katherine went to the police station on 82nd Street, the same place where, not so long afterward, her death certificate and her autopsy reports would go, and she asked to speak to someone. She was told to go upstairs and there she walked along the bright metal corridor to the squad room where Tom Cooley and Louie McBride worked. She was introduced to Detective Thompson.

She wanted to report an assault and attempted robbery, she said.

One month later Freddie was arrested, but the judge dismissed the charges.

After filing the complaint Katherine walked home to 72nd Street. She looked at her apartment with the sofa bed and the rows of books, the red candles in the window, and the frying pans on the stove. It took over a week for the purple swelling around her eye to disappear and she didn't talk to Linda much anymore. They still met in the hallways and down on the street and Linda would stop to talk and let her know they could be friends, but Katherine was different, Linda said. She turned away from her and she seemed preoccupied.

"It wasn't like her," Linda remembered. "I never knew much about her personal life or her family, but I wondered about her, especially with what happened after that.

"It must have been ten days or two weeks later when we heard the same sounds again in her room. There were crashes and bangings around and sometimes voices."

Charlie and Linda listened and they talked about what they thought was happening. But they didn't go out in the hall or rush next door to see if they could help.

"She didn't need help," Linda said. "It was what she wanted."

"After that," the young woman continued, "it happened a lot. Every two weeks or so. And it got so Charlie and I would just turn over in bed and say, 'Katherine's at it again.' It always sounded like a fight. I guess it was some kind of rough sex. Some people get off on that and she must have had to be raped or kicked around or something to feel any excitement or thrill. But," she added, "what could we do?"

Katherine told very few people at that time or at any time what was really happening to her and very few people saw her enough to know what was happening. Furthermore, many of the people she did see didn't care enough to notice much. All in all she was protected and obscured by herself.

But still, there was a change in twenty-seven-year-old

Katherine Cleary. The change was barely visible, camou-
flaged, and yet its general path there had to be seen and
traced.

Cooley and McBride got a lot of information about
Katherine Cleary but they didn't want to talk about this
aspect of her life, they said. It wasn't their business, her
sex life and what she did was up to her. They weren't the
ones who would talk about it. "Don't expect Irish cops to
tell you the truth about Katherine Cleary or any woman,"
a pathologist in the case said later. "They only want to
protect women, especially an Irish woman, and guard
their reputations."

But not all people felt that sense of obligation toward
Katherine Cleary. Other people did talk. They weren't up
in the apartment and they didn't hear any of the sounds
of violence or anger. But for the first time they said they
saw Katherine Cleary with men who were conspicuously
beneath her. Rough and unattractive men, who weren't
her social equal, her mental equal, or her equal at anything, they said. They saw her begin to spend time in
places like the Green Oaks Bar, standing up at the counter
talking to the kind of folks some people avoid in the subway. And they saw her walking down the street with them
and then, they said, taking them home. She used to hook
up largely with men who were as anonymous as herself,
sweet and innocuous. Now she sometimes had men who
were actually conspicuous. They were the real debris of an
urban society.

There was another change, people said. It was no
longer just the Katherine Cleary who was sweet and well-
mannered, if sometimes too loud and brash. It was a

woman who was bitchy, a woman who turned on these new partners with nastiness and contempt. She bantered and played and derided; she let someone approach and then pushed him back. They saw her with the lines of teasing and control, manipulation and meanness in her hands for once.

And they saw her like it, enjoy it. They could only guess at what happened in private, or if these men occasionally retaliated. And they could only guess at why Katherine wanted—or at least got—that abuse and pain. Maybe, perhaps, she thought it was her due.

"I tried to warn her," Linda said, "but you could tell she'd gotten into it. She changed. She began hanging around with undesirable types, rough, tough people. I'd see her in bars and she always seemed to go after the street people.

"There are some pretty racy girls around here," Linda said, "and they get the better guys. You know what it's like to live on an open street like this, but Katherine couldn't make it with those kind of guys. She didn't have it together enough. Charlie: He never liked her. He said she made him nervous. She had too much head and he thought she was always cutting him down.

"She just didn't have enough style or poise to attract the good men and she had a way of going after the unsavory types. She gravitated toward people in the same kind of loser syndrome as she. And I said to her time and again, whenever I had the chance, 'You pick up that type, Katherine, and you're asking for trouble.' 'I know,' she'd say, 'I'm not stupid.' 'Certain people you stay away from.'

" 'Oh, yes, I'll be careful,' she'd say.

"But she wasn't. She must have found what she wanted."

WHEN JOE WILLIE left New York with Danny's clothes and hundred-dollar bills, he flew to Miami. There he telephoned J. Philip Wallerstein from the airport.

"Come on over," Phil said. "Me and my partner, Jack, we got a house. We got an extra room, too, just for you."

It was November 1971. Joe Willie moved in with his suitcase and his clothes and not long afterward the front door opened one day and Carole Musty walked in. She was with her girlfriend and she was barefoot.

She was tall and olive-skinned. She had long thick dark hair, a flat belly and little breasts and pubic hair that curled out around the edges of her short shorts. She sat down and curled her bare legs up beneath her like a cat and was quiet. She was sixteen years old.

Phil asked her what grade she was in and she said, "Tenth."

Joe Willie asked her if she wanted a beer and she nodded. She was sitting on the couch wrapping her hair around her ear with her finger and dangling it through her mouth.

Joe Willie handed her the beer and watched her. She took a swallow and put the can in her lap between her legs.

Then he sat down next to her and put his arm up behind her. After a while he took a piece of the long hair in his hand and felt it. He rubbed it up and down as if it were a piece of lovely material, then he looked at her and smiled. He was feeling things he'd never felt before.

"Nice," he said. "Nice hair."

She looked at him and smiled, too. "Thanks," she said.

Several hours later she followed Joe Willie into the bathroom and then the bedroom and after that she followed him to Viola Camp, to New York, and to his future. They had very little in common, but they loved each other. Joe Willie, for one, liked her body and liked the way she was. She always said, "I don't care" and, "It doesn't matter to me," and she never questioned him or doubted his rights. She was like a thing of nature that thrived and did not think and with her slow-moving dark eyes she had no dreams or ambitions, so Joe Willie gave her his and in his barren desert world she became his future.

Carole Musty for her part talks about it all now in the same spirit of apathy and indifference Joe Willie found so attractive. She is older now and no longer looks like a child, but she still has the panoramic eyes that see but never judge. She drinks glasses of Tab and talks like someone lying on the beach who is too hot and drowsy to move.

"I was living at home with my parents in a trailer in South Miami," she said, "and one day my girlfriend said to me, 'Let's skip school. I want to take you out to this house to drink some beer and have a good time,' and I said, 'Okay.' So we went and Joe Willie and these guys named Phil and Jack were living there. There was loads of beer and money all over the tables and they didn't look like they were the kind of people that could really have that much money and everyone was introducing everyone else.

"To tell the truth, I didn't really care. I was just sixteen and out to find someone to have a good time with and Joe Willie was as good as anybody. My friend wasn't really his girlfriend, she was just somebody he was screwing, and right away I could tell he liked me. He was very attractive and paid a lot of attention to me. It was like he was saying, 'I want to go to bed with you now, but I really like you, too.' Which was kinda nice. It didn't really matter to me, so we ended up going to bed and it didn't bother me at all and as it turned out we started seeing more and more of each other.

"I was infatuated with the way they did things," she went on, "with everything about Joe Willie and them, with how they robbed and had a good time, and how we would all pile in the car and go to the drive-in and get totally loaded on beer and dope. It was very different than anything I'd ever done before.

"I had gone to bed with other guys before just for the hell of it, but Joe Willie was something out of the ordinary. He would have given me the moon on a silver platter. The guys said he was bisexual or homosexual, but it didn't matter to me. He treated me like I was the queen of the world and he was great as far as sex is concerned. I've never known anyone who cared as much as he did to give me everything with sex. He loved it and he taught me as much as he could. He wanted me to understand the full meaning of it and that anything and everything, as long as two people consent, is great.

"That whole time of November and December," she

went on, "was very exciting. There was money and danger and thrills and I remember one night Joe Willie got out of bed and said, 'Wait here. We'll be home about four o'clock in the morning.' And they came home with sacks of change and we spilled it out on the floor and rolled in the nickels and dimes and quarters. They had hit a restaurant, after hours, and taken cases and cases of beer and loose change and tons of steaks. They never did an armed robbery. Usually they would go into people's homes and take teevees and stereos. We had quite a few nice color teevees."

Joe Willie hadn't told her very much about himself, but he did tell her about Danny Murray. He was his best friend, he said.

BACK IN NEW YORK Danny Murray was losing weight. He wanted to sell his apartment and move, but every time he looked at the ads in the classified he remembered Joe Willie. Every time he came home, he wondered if Joe Willie would be there and every time he went to bed at night or woke up in the morning, his battles with himself revolved around the pain that Joe Willie had left behind. He felt rejected, angry, hurt, humiliated, and sad. He swallowed Valiums, aspirins and TV dinners and it never occurred to him he'd see Joe Willie Simpson again.

On December first the telephone rang. "Hello," he said.

"Hi." It was Joe Willie. "How you doing?"

His voice was light and airy, the same as always. He sounded as if they had talked that morning and were going to meet in a few minutes, and Danny heard it. It told him something. "I'm fine," he said slowly. "How are you?"

"Fine. I been thinking about you a whole lot."

Danny didn't answer. It was like dying, he said later, the whole jumble of thoughts and feelings rushing through his head as if they'd never have another chance. He was relieved, and exhilarated, but still suspicious, watchful. "I should have been furious with him and screamed and yelled and said, 'I'm going to get you,' " he said later, "but instead I gradually became totally calm, totally at ease, as if my whole life had slipped back into shape again."

"Hey," Joe Willie said, "you're not mad at me, are you? Why aren't you saying anything?" He stopped. "Are you mad?"

"No. Should I be?"

"I don't think so. Hey," he said, "hold on a second, will you?" He put down the phone and there was silence. Then, after a minute or two, he came back on the line. "I want you to meet Carole," he said. "Carole," he directed, "say 'Hi.' This is Danny. Danny. You know Danny. My best friend. Say 'Hi' to him."

Then he put Carole on the line.

"Hello." The girl's voice came slow through the receiver. "Joe Willie sure talks about you a lot. How are you?"

"I'm fine," Danny said, and suddenly he felt excited and happy. "How are you? You sound like you're having fun."

"We are," the girl drawled. "We're in bed. We been here for hours. Joe Willie, we got to get up," she said to the side. "We got to eat something."

Joe Willie got back on the phone. "That's Carole," he said proudly to Danny. "Carole Musty."

"She sounds really nice," Danny said. "And you sound terrific, Joe Willie. I guess everything's all right?"

"Oh, everything's wonderful," Joe Willie said. "Just wonderful."

"You're in Miami. Right?"

"Yes."

"That's what I figured somehow. Are you working?"

"Well, not exactly, but I got a thing going with Phil. Remember Phil Wallerstein I told you about? He and I got a setup here. It's not legal but I promise you, Danny, it's totally safe. I don't want you to worry. It's totally safe. Nothing can go wrong. We're really operating just great."

"Well, be careful. It can't be all that safe if it's not legal. But I'm glad you're in good shape. I'm really glad to hear from you, Joe Willie. I didn't know what happened to you. You just disappeared. Remember?"

"Ya, I know," said Joe Willie. "But I've been busy. I meant to give you a call before but I just didn't get around to it. Wait until you meet Carole," he added, "you'll just love her. She's the greatest girl in the world, Danny, you just won't believe how wonderful she is."

"I'm really happy for you," Danny said.

"Okay, well, listen," Joe Willie said. "I'll call you again. We got to get up and go get something to eat."

A few days later he called again. This time the call was collect. The conversation lasted about forty-five minutes and at one point Joe Willie said, "You didn't do anything about those Christmas orders, did you?"

Earlier in New York he and Danny had chosen Christmas presents for the entire Simpson family from a mail order catalogue and, finished, Joe Willie turned to Danny and said, "Can I put these on your Master Charge?"

Danny said yes. "I thought it was wonderful he felt enough for his family to think of buying them something," he told a friend.

Now, three weeks before Christmas, Joe Willie was checking on the order.

"I canceled them," Danny said.

"You canceled them?" Joe Willie repeated in obvious surprise. "What'd you do that for?"

"After you left the way you did, I thought that was only fair."

"Oh, Danny, why'd you do that? You should have known better. You should have known I wouldn't really leave you or hurt you. That was just something I had to do to get away."

Several days later Joe Willie called again. Danny accepted the call and this time Joe Willie had a favor to ask. He wanted Danny to pick up his suitcases in storage and ship them to Miami.

Danny spent the whole afternoon on the project. He went to the storage company, lugged the bags by taxi to the bus station, and waited in line for what seemed like hours to ship them south.

"I'll never forget it," he said later. "It was one of the

happiest days of my life. I couldn't get over how much he trusted me."

JOE WILLIE AND PHIL and Jack hadn't given all that much thought to what they were doing between the hours of midnight and dawn, but the Miami police had. While they figured the thieves weren't making more than $150 a night, they sure were a hell of a nuisance, and for some time now they had been sticking pins in a map to mark all the places where the televisions had been.

And then one night the robbery squad was waiting outside one of those little bungalows and as Joe Willie came out the rear window, his arms full, the cops shined their wide-angle light high and found him. His suitcases had only just arrived from New York, but the Gold Coast pleasure spree was already over.

Joe Willie went into the back seat of a police car and headed off to spend his first night in jail. He would not like it.

Phil and Jack managed to escape. They returned to the apartment, where Carole and a girl named Janie were asleep on the couch. Afraid of being arrested, they all piled in a car and drove north. When they arrived in New York, they panhandled for several days and then Phil telephoned Daniel P. Murray.

First he introduced himself. Then he said, "We got all your clothes and stuff Joe Willie took. We'll sell it back to you for a hundred bucks."

Danny agreed to meet them in a parking lot near Madison Square Garden. He was curious about Carole, but she was tired and didn't say much. He bought his clothes, learned as much as possible about Joe Willie's situation, and gave them an extra fifty dollars to live on. They left for Toronto, saying they'd stay in touch.

Meanwhile Joe Willie's bail was set at ten thousand dollars. Danny called a friend in Miami named Dick Sylvester. Dick was a lawyer and he went to work on Joe Willie's case. Out in Viola Camp, the Simpsons borrowed enough money to post bond and on December twenty-third Joe Willie was released from jail.

He was alone, depressed, and Danny sent him money to go home for Christmas. Afterward he flew on to New York to stay with his friend on the thirty-second floor. The lawyer Sylvester had arranged for him to plead guilty on March first to a reduced robbery charge and now all Joe Willie had to do was make a decision. He didn't know whether to face sentencing and go to jail, or forfeit the bail and run.

He hated the thought of jail. He wanted to run.

"He was in a terrible blue period," Danny said. "It had never occurred to him he would get in trouble because, the way he saw it, those robberies weren't hurting anybody and he never dreamed he'd have to face any consequences. He was very depressed," Danny went on, "and all the time he kept saying, 'I'm never going back, I'm never going back,' but then as March first got closer and closer, guilt got the better of him. The key question was letting his parents down. If he didn't show up in court they'd lose their money and he felt he was enough of a disappointment to them already. In the end he decided it was better to be in jail than to let them down even more.

"On the twenty-seventh, Joe Willie returned to Miami. He stayed in a hotel and phoned me every hour. He was desperate. The twenty-ninth of February about ten o'-clock at night he called again.

"Tomorrow was the big day, and I said, 'Joe Willie, you know, I really feel bad about all this and if it would solve anything or help, I'd come down just to be with you, but you never asked me for help.'

"He was really surprised. It never occurred to him to ask for help directly. But this time he said, 'I'm asking you. Please. Come.'

"And I said, 'Okay, I'll be there.'

"I hung up the phone and with no clothes or anything, grabbed some money and my credit cards and went right to the airport. He was to be in court by ten and the plane was grounded by fog, but I finally arrived in Miami and took a cab straight to the court.

"He was already before the judge. They'd even taken his belt off, as a protection against suicide, I guess, and were about to take him off to prison, when something happened and the word came out from his lawyer Sylvester that the sentencing had been postponed and that he might even get probation later on.

"Well," Danny said, "you have never in your life seen such an ecstatic boy. He was stunned. He was whooping and screaming and jumping up and down. He couldn't believe it. For once something had turned out right."

35

DANNY AND JOE WILLIE and the lawyer Sylvester went to lunch to celebrate. Joe Willie ordered filet mignon and then excused himself to go to the bathroom.

Time passed. The two men talked and then Danny looked at his watch. Joe Willie had been gone thirty minutes. "Something's wrong," he said.

"You'd better find him," Sylvester said.

Danny rushed through the dining room to the men's room. It was empty except for Joe Willie. He was sitting on a chair crying, his head bent over in his arms and his body shaking with sobs.

"Oh, Joe Willie," Danny said, as he closed the door and went over to him. He put his arms around the boy and rubbed his shoulders. "It's all right," he murmured. "Everything's going to be all right now."

The boy went on crying and crying and then gradually he started to catch his breath. Then he suddenly said, "I'm so happy. I can't believe it. I've got another chance, Danny," he blurted out. "I'm so happy and now everything's gonna be all right." He straightened up and wiped the tears off his face. "I know it is."

He looked at Danny. "I'm going to do everything now," he said, "and all my plans are going to come true."

"That's right," Danny said.

"Everything's gonna work now."

Danny nodded.

"And you know the first thing I'm going to do?" Joe Willie said as he stood up and tucked his shirt in.

"What?"

He looked proud, even defiant, his shoulders straight, his head high. "I'm going to tell Carole's parents that I'm going to marry her. I'm not even going to ask. I'm going to tell them. I'm going to marry her just as soon as I can. No ifs, ands, or buts."

"He came and told my father, 'I'm here to get Carole,' and we went out and rode around on a motorcycle he'd borrowed from the lawyer Sylvester, and Joe Willie was excited and I was thrilled, and we wanted to get married. Joe Willie always had dreams, big, high dreams. He wanted to be a success. He wanted to be out there in front, on top. A man. And we thought his time had come. 'I'll go far with this guy,' I thought. 'He has real goals and real ambitions.' One time he said he was going to be a salesman and another time he was going to go to school and get a degree and he always said, 'We'll have a nice house and kids,' and I thought, 'Wow, it sounds great.' And he said, 'I'm going to make a lot of money for you.' And I believed him. I thought his time had come and so did he."

36

EIGHT DAYS LATER, on March ninth, Joe Willie Simpson and Carole Musty stood up in the corner of the Hotel Vagabond in Miami under a gold fleur-de-lis that hung from the wall and they were married in a double-ring ceremony.

Danny Murray was there. He bought the rings. "I thought it was the best thing that ever happened to Joe Willie," he said. "It was the first time I'd ever seen him really happy. I'd never seriously thought I could ever have him all to myself, so to speak, and I really thought marriage would give him all the stability and happiness he needed."

The Simpsons came from Viola Camp and the Mustys drove up from their trailer in the south. The night before the wedding, they all stayed at the hotel and about ten thirty the Simpsons went to bed. Carole left with a girlfriend and Joe Willie turned to Danny and said, "Come on. Let's go for a ride."

They went outside the hotel and got on the back of the motorcycle Joe Willie had borrowed from Sylvester. They went through the city streets and down a highway that led out into the country. There, beneath the stars and the hot dark sky, they drove long and fast and hard.

Danny's ears whistled and his head was light. He held

Joe Willie tight around the stomach. The bike reached one hundred and twenty miles an hour and Danny thought to himself: "If it all ends right here, it's been worth it."

The next morning he and Joe Willie and Dick had breakfast in a shopping center. Joe Willie vomited in the bathroom and apologized for being nervous and fidgety. Afterward Danny went out to buy the rings. He found two gold bands inlaid with diamonds, and at four thirty that afternoon he stood alongside Joe Willie and Carole Musty in the hotel lobby. He was the best man.

The Lutheran pastor raised his hand and said the words and all the friends listened and Marjorie Simpson cried in happiness and Carole wore a short white dress that showed her knees and was scooped out low around the neck. Joe Willie was wearing a suit colored smoky-blue that he bought with money from Danny, and he had a silk tie two inches wide with a dark blue stripe down the middle.

Afterward the group gathered in a corner of the dining room. There was champagne and a cake and everyone was happy. Joe Willie and Carole showed their rings and kissed and they all gave toasts to prosperity and babies and the forever after. The future was there in that red velvet room with the glass chandelier and the tin ashtrays, and it was rolled out like a carpet in front of the twenty-two-year-old groom. His hair was combed and wet for the occasion and he went around the room putting his arm around everyone and telling each one in turn, and in secret, that he or she was the one who had helped him the most, the one he loved the best.

There are pictures of all this, dozens of three-by-five color prints in a matte finish, of the cake and the champagne and the headwaiter; pictures of the bride and groom, the young couple with his parents, and then her parents, and others of all of them together. And now they are stored in the box beneath Sue Ann's bed in Viola Camp.

37

AFTERWARD JOE WILLIE and Carole went to live in the guest room at Dick Sylvester's house until, they said, they "really" got settled. Carole did the housework and Joe Willie did the odd jobs and although he thought a lot about his plans, the next court date kept coming closer and closer. It was set for the end of May and two weeks before, Danny came down to visit.

He rented a car at the airport and moved into the other guest room at Dick's. They all ate and played and talked and then on Sunday afternoon Joe Willie drove away in Danny's car and didn't come back.

The next day there was still no sign of him. They reported the car stolen, but said they had no idea who took it. Days passed and then, back in New York, Danny got a letter from a Holiday Inn in northwest Florida. It was three pages long and had been written "Sunday, on road."

"Sorry I felt I had to steal your car and cause you the trouble," Joe Willie wrote, "but yours was the only one to take without stealing from someone."

He had decided to run away, he said, because, "I'm going to prison for sure and I don't want to chance losing Carole." He was writing Danny, he said, to outline his plans. "I'm relying completely on my belief that you are the only one who is honest about helping Carole and I and that you will trust my judgment completely."

> My plan is this: I am going to a place I used to live out West. [This, he later said, was Winnemucca.] "Everyone's forgotten I traveled all over and no one will know where to look. I know where to get work and am going to. I am getting false I.D. and am getting an apartment in this little town I know. I am counting on you for Carole, yours and my future, so please believe me and convince Carole to come and be with me. I love Carole dearly and if I have to lose her I'll die. In about a week or two I'll send for her. This is the only way. I know we can live and be happy in a new place as man and wife. It's a small town where I won't get stopped by the police once I get known. I'm positive it'll work or I wouldn't be doing it. I'd call you to talk to you, but I'm afraid you might try to talk me out of this and I have to keep exactly to my plan or it won't work. PLEASE TRUST ME. I need you now. Joe Willie.

Several days later Joe Willie Simpson returned to Miami. He walked in the door of the lawyer's house and said, "Hello." He didn't mention Winnemucca or his plans or running away. He didn't say much of anything. He just sat down and waited for prison.

That came a few days later when the judge sentenced

him to one year in the county stockade. He said good-bye
to Carole and left. Carole took a job as a maid in Coral
Gables and Joe Willie was signed into jail where he was
told to wash dishes, sleep on a bunk, and listen to lectures
on alcoholism. As soon as he could he went to the com-
missary. He bought cigarettes, a ballpoint pen, and a pad
of white paper. Then he went back to his cell and he wrote
his first letter to Danny.

"Buddy," it began. "You've probably heard, but I made
out great in court. Only one year."

That was a Friday.

Friday night he wrote again, and said:

All in all I feel very good about the profits that I personally made the insane last few months. Look at the gains: (1)
I learned the feeling and true meaning of friendship, love,
hate, sympathy. PRICELESS. (2) I was able to marry the most
valuable treasure on earth, Carole. EXTREMELY PRICELESS.
(3) You and I, in my opinion, passed from an awkward,
removed relationship to a love so strong that if you need
my life, it is yours. (4) I am now a man to my parents which
is one goal every male seeks. (5) When I finish this time [in
jail] my life will be squared up enough to start a fresh, new
exciting life with Carole. I hope you will join us and be with
us forever.

When this year or two whatever [in jail] is over, I plan
to work long enough to buy a V.W. bus, save some money
and take off and show Carole this country, working here
and there, taking plenty of time and then when we're
ready, settling down somewhere. I sincerely hope you will
join us on our trip. I plan to stop here and there taking
whatever work I can and not only seeing this beautiful

country but also living each part of it as we go. I would go as far as to beg you to come with us but maybe I've talked you into too much as it is. I will just say this: it wouldn't be half as great without you, so please consider it.

On Sunday he wrote Danny again. His handwriting is neat, with large round curves and a slant to the back. At the end he said:

> Within two years after I'm out [of jail] I'll have my own business, you'll see. I never worked to get ahead before because I didn't care, but now I do. You're going to see things happening. Just think how much I've done since I met Carole. I'm going to be able to really turn on after I get this out of the way and then watch out world. I know my capabilities and the sky's the limit. Within five years after I get out I'll be making at least thirty-five thousand dollars a year. I know it. And you have to be with us, please.

The letters continued every few days, but a mood of depression began to settle in and, at the end of one letter, on June 21, he wrote: "I feel so alone, if anyone ever felt as though all the cards had been dealt against them, it's me."

Three letters later, on June 28, he said:

> For supposedly being such a con man, I sure am still locked up tighter than hell. I start working in the laundry in the morning. Great, huh? Screwed again. I'm trying to do this like a man and keep being treated like a dog. Things had better change or I'm going to change them.

His last letter came on a Tuesday in July:

> This cell is like a walking morgue, a real bunch of born losers, mostly Cubans, twelve of us, four blacks, five Cubans, and three whites. Keeping my spirits up is a constant ordeal. I'm so darn horny it hurts.

A few days later Danny got a telephone call from Joe Willie. He was in a phone booth in downtown Miami; he had run lickety-split down the prison recreation yard and taken a flying leap over the walls. He exchanged his jail clothes for a pair of pants in a garbage dump and now he didn't know what to do. As usual, Danny told him.

After they hung up the telephone, Danny went to the airlines office and bought two one-way tickets on the ten-o'clock flight from Miami to New York. The tickets were to be picked up in Miami, he said. At the same time, Joe Willie, with Danny's credit card number, ordered flowers to be delivered to Carole Musty. Several hours later he called her. He had panhandled for the dime.

"Where are you?" she asked. "Why did you send the flowers? What's going on?"

"I can't talk now," he said. "Just hurry. Meet me at the airport. National Airlines. As soon as possible."

So, as Mr. and Mrs. John Maxwell, they picked up their tickets at the airport that hot summer night and two hours later, penniless and depressed, the young couple arrived in New York City. They went to live with Danny Murray in his penthouse apartment on the thirty-second floor.

38

IT WAS THE SUMMER of 1972 and Joe Willie Simpson and Katherine Cleary now lived three blocks apart. Hot wind blew across the rivers and settled on the city, and the days were long and the nights short. The air was full of steam and smells and men with aprons and pushcarts roamed the streets selling popsicles and pinwheels. It was the season for melons and baseball and over on the West Side people sat on their stoops in the heat and listened to the radio.

High above the city on the thirty-second floor Joe Willie shut off the air conditioner and at night the long, heavy blue curtains swayed against the floor as a breeze pushed into the room. Carole lay on her back beside him and out in the living room Danny was wrapped in a sheet on the couch.

At Two-Five-Three, the doorman sat in a folding chair in the sun on the sidewalk and Katherine teased him that that was no way to work, and he said the heat was no time to work. It was the weather for sundresses and halters and bikinis, but Katherine looked at her silhouette in the bathroom glass and stayed with her blouses and skirts. On vacations before, she had skied and gone to Europe, been to the mountains and visited friends in Ohio. But this summer she stayed in the place she knew best, and with no longer any difference between the weekdays and the weekends, she waited up late and talked long and got to know the shutters and the metal doors of 72nd Street as if they were the walls of her own home.

It was on one of these days that Katherine Cleary met Jefferson Thomas Williams at Tweed's and began to go back with him to his house or hers. He was black and large, at least a foot taller than she, and he drove a Cadillac with tail fins and bright colors and wore a broad-brimmed hat. He smoked long thin cigars and had a quiet voice.

People in Tweed's knew Jefferson Thomas Williams might be anything from a pimp to a bank teller to a dope dealer, but they also knew that the women he chose were small and white and smart, and so it was no surprise, really, that he picked Katherine. He was also, apparently, a very kind man, and it was thought that he would appreciate and understand the sometimes lost and troubled ways of the little schoolteacher.

DANNY KEPT HIS ALARM clock, pillow, and Kleenex in the living room, and Joe Willie and Carole were ensconced in the bedroom. They bought lots of food for the kitchen and took out subscriptions to *Reader's Digest* and *Screen Life, Time, Newsweek* and *Popular Mechanics.* With Danny they learned the lines to songs from *Funny Girl* and

Cabaret and sang to each other at home and on the street.

Weeks passed. They went to movies and they walked hand in hand with Carole in the middle. They bought hot dogs outside the Museum of Natural History and they went out late at night to get ice cream cones. Miami and the Dade County Stockade seemed a long way away and in New York time stopped and the summer heat took over. They all loved each other very much. They went on the Staten Island Ferry and showed Carole the Club Forty-six. They played riddles and invented games and wore T-shirts and if Joe Willie ever remembered things like the long gray building in Madison or the ragged bloody marks along his arm or wondered where his plans went next, there was a lull of time there that summer of 1972 when he did seem free.

They all did. The time was a present.

Jeff and Katherine met together on and off and in time he told her that he was not a pimp or a bank teller or a dealer, but an airline pilot. Some people said afterward that she too shared a secret with him and let him know what she had started to do with her nights from time to time. The way she explained it, people said, she would begin in a mood of defiance, even revenge—I'll get you, world—but then afterward be left with nothing but shame and disgust.

Jeff was kind, people said. He told her it wasn't bad and she wasn't bad and she shouldn't feel guilty.

Far away in Miami, Hank and Iona Musty talked about their daughter and Joe Willie. Hank didn't think Joe Willie was a bad kid; he just thought he was mixed up and needed to get himself together.

Out in Viola Camp, Marjorie Simpson hoped marriage would give Joe Willie the stability he needed.

Danny, for his part, had always known he couldn't keep Joe Willie to himself, but now he hoped he could keep Joe Willie and Carole both. He fantasized often about them all spending their lives together and having one home or two but a life that was intermingled and a life that gave him the family he'd always wanted. He wanted the best for Joe Willie and wanted him to be independent and financially stable, but some part of him also knew that as long as Joe Willie didn't really make it or head out on his own, he, Danny, had a better chance of being in the picture.

"I know I was doing a lot for Joe Willie—and for Carole, too—but I got a lot back in return. He made me happy. He made me secure. He made me feel I was needed," he said, "and that I could do anything in the world I wanted. He made me feel I belonged. To him. And to Carole."

CAROLE AND JOE WILLIE had no money at all. Danny paid all the bills and one day Joe Willie said he was thinking of going back to work. Everybody knew what he meant. It didn't mean going to an office or getting a paycheck.

"It's really getting to me," he said. "I'm supposed to be a man; I got a wife and I'm supposed to look after her, but instead I'm running from the law and living off my best friend."

He couldn't get food stamps or welfare because he was a fugitive and he had no identification cards to show for a job. His only recourse, he said, was the same one as before.

He asked Carole what she thought.

"It doesn't matter to me," Carole said. "It's not like you'd be cheating on me. You're doing it for money and as long as I'm getting fed, I don't care."

"If it's going to make you feel better," Danny told him next, "I think you should do it."

Joe Willie went to the phone and called the number. The woman on the other end of the line didn't remember him until he reminded her of the jobs he had taken and the places he had gone. He mentioned the townhouse on the East Side where the man liked to lie in a coffin in the dark and be frightened, but never touched, and he mentioned the man who did like to be touched, with lighted cigarettes on the end of his penis, and the other man who wanted to be tied down with ropes and raped in the rear like a woman.

Mostly what he did, though, Joe Willie reminded her, was just the regular stuff.

The woman said fine. She took his phone number and he began to get calls.

The way Carole remembers it, the calls came in the afternoon or the evening and sometimes he was gone for an hour, sometimes all night. "It would depend on how far he had to travel and what he did when he was there," she said. "He would be at home watching television and someone would call and he'd go out. Danny and I would stay and play cards and watch teevee, and he'd come home later and put the money out on the table. And tell us what he had to do. It wasn't bad stuff," she said, "only sometimes he had to do the business with cigarettes, but mostly he just laid back and took whatever the guy gave him. He got like fifty to seventy-five dollars per guy for a quick session.

"He was real casual talking about it," she added. "He wasn't ashamed or anything. I think he thought he was smart to take advantage of his talents."

41

PEOPLE UP AND DOWN 72nd Street remember Katherine Cleary that summer, but they talked about the little person in skirts and blue jeans two different ways, as if she were either loud and "looking for action," or else back somewhere in the shadows with a book or a quiet friend. They began to speak of her now as two people, the one or the other.

"She was a bizarre woman," said one man who knew her well and could have had a lot to say. "She was strange but she knew what she liked." That last year, he said, a change came over her like a cloud.

But, he said, he wasn't going to say anymore. "She's gone now," he said, "and I'm not going to sully her memory. I'm not going to be the one who talks about it."

"I never knew Katherine Cleary," another person, a woman, said. "All I know was I saw her around the neighborhood. I used to see her in places I wouldn't want to go and she was with men I wouldn't want to be with. But I don't know anything about her."

IT WAS ONE OF THOSE hot autumn nights when lightning flashed in the western sky that Joe Willie turned over in bed toward the flat little breasts of Carole and did with her what he often did.

But on one of those nights, while Danny was asleep beyond the open door, Carole took more of Joe Willie than she or he had wanted and later the doctor wrote in his report that she was pregnant.

"After a while Joe Willie stopped hustling," Carole said. "We found out I was pregnant. I went to a doctor and he gave me a test and right away Joe Willie stopped with the men. He said it wasn't fitting.

"Danny agreed. He said he'd help us out moneywise.

"I said I didn't know what difference a baby made, but Joe Willie got angry. He said it made a difference to him. He said he had to be a family man."

43

KATHERINE DECIDED TO spend some time in Holyoke. She lay in blue jeans out on the lawn and stared up at the sky and listened to the birds. Her mother joined her there and they ate tomato sandwiches and talked. The neighbors came and cousins came, and everybody talked and these afternoons spread into the evening and the conversations were good and after a while the neighbors and the cousins left. And Katherine and her parents talked on into the night. The words flowed between Vincent Cleary and his grown-up daughter and they were about politics and the economy, his work and her work, and about life itself. Mary Cleary watched, listened, and talked, too, and she must have felt good.

She told someone later that she knew very little "actually" about her daughter's life in New York City, and sometimes, she indicated, she looked at her daughter and she wondered what she did back in that hard world of concrete and elevators, and sometimes she feared for Katherine. She didn't really know why, she said. It wasn't as if anything had happened and she certainly had no feeling anything would happen, but sometimes her daughter seemed so small and New York so large, and all her deep maternal feeling would want to reach out and grab her back.

But life was good for Vincent and Mary Cleary. All the

years of raising three children were over and now there was space and money and time and the fruits of the years before were coming back in every way.

And as for Katherine, Mrs. Cleary said, "She seemed to want to be around us. Things were good between us and I think they were getting better. But I knew she was very unhappy."

THE BABY WAS DUE in May 1973.

As a first step toward finding a job, Joe Willie got a library card under another name. Then he got some more cards and then he started job hunting. He answered ads and went to agencies, but every day he came back to the thirty-second floor discouraged. He sat in front of the television set in his undershorts and drank bourbon long into the night. He rarely talked at all.

Occasionally he began to tell Danny he could sleep in the bed with him. "Carole, you sleep on the couch tonight," he'd say.

"I have to repay him somehow," he explained to her, "and this is all I have to give him. The sex means nothing to me, but it really means a lot to him."

"He was right in a way," Danny said afterward. "It did mean a lot to me. But I'd never have asked. I wanted their marriage to work."

"I didn't mind," Carole said. "Danny was his best

friend, but I knew he was using him. He used everybody, that's the way he was. He needed Danny more and according to his way of thinking, that meant he had to pay him back more. Sex was all he thought he had to give, I guess. But he always manipulated people to get what he wanted. We all knew that, even Danny, and we all knew too that he really loved me. So how could I be jealous? Besides," she added, "I liked Danny, too."

"He was the only person in the world who ever made me happy," Danny said one night when he sat staring into a cup of coffee. "I don't understand how he did it, but he had the capacity to wrench me out of myself and make me come alive. He turned everything into an adventure. I remember once we went to Coney Island and we didn't do much of anything, just walked along and went on some rides. But it was one of the most exciting days of my life.

"He was the one with the troubles, but he made everyone else happy."

SOMETIME THAT FALL Katherine went to a psychiatrist. The question of whether to do this had been on her mind for quite a while but there is no way of knowing whether she talked freely and openly with him, the way she found so difficult with her friends. Or whether she was reticent and full of jokes. Did she tell him about her past, and the one year that lasted a lifetime? Did she talk about her life on 72nd Street? She must, at least, have said that sometimes she thought she was fine, but other times she thought she was going crazy.

And who knows what the doctor said. He might have been the kind who believed—as she herself feared—that marriage and a family were the only satisfactions for a woman, or he may have looked beyond that question and focused instead on her own shifting, failing sense of herself.

He did one thing, though, that not all psychiatrists do. He prescribed pills. He wrote out a prescription for a mood equalizer and Katherine took the medicine for a while. "I'm finally getting myself together," she told one woman.

The woman listened, but didn't believe her. "She just thought she was getting better," she said.

Not long afterward Katherine told her she had stopped seeing the psychiatrist. She said she couldn't afford it.

But the woman saw it differently. She talked about Katherine one night when the rain was coming down hard and the city streets were ablaze with lights and reflections and she pictured Katherine as unable to hold herself together anymore. It was as if pieces of her life, like chunks of meteors, were breaking off and falling away. "She tried to convince everyone she was strong," she said, "but everything was slipping."

46

IN LATE SEPTEMBER, Joe Willie got a job as a mail clerk in the basement of a midtown office building.

He made one hundred and six dollars a week.

After taxes and social security were taken out, he had ninety-two dollars to take back to the thirty-second floor, or, as he saw it, three hundred and sixty-eight dollars a month for himself, his bride, his baby, a home, rent, and food. He already owed the employment agency one hundred dollars and the obstetrician four hundred dollars. The doctor wanted it as a down payment, or, as he put it, "security."

Joe Willie and Carole and Danny played pool almost every night at Broadway Billiards near Times Square. It was a smoky basement cavern crowded with green felt tables, and on one wall there was a board with names like Luther Lassiter and Minnesota Fats written in gold. Often they talked about those distant figures and wondered just how good they were and then, inevitably, they'd get around to the imaginary game when one of them would play against Fats himself.

It was fun and it was worth a laugh, but it was like a lot of things in their life.

Like the ranch.

There was a ranch in their life. They hadn't found it yet, but it was out west somewhere and right now it belonged to someone else. In the future, though, they were going to buy it, and the three of them and their children were going to live there. It was their future.

The only thing was, though, it wasn't happening and they never did get into a game with Minnesota Fats. And that fall the dreams just weren't working and it looked as if Joe Willie Simpson was beginning to suspect that nothing would.

There were plenty of signs. At first he just found it difficult to get up in the morning but then he began to call in sick. And as he got worse, he wouldn't eat dinner. He just took off his clothes, sat in front of the television set in his undershorts, and drank, and the hours went by like a silent marching parade.

Later it got so he came home from work early and would sit on the couch drinking and staring out over the Hudson River for hours. In the distance were the hills and the sky, but that didn't matter because he wasn't looking and he wasn't seeing.

KATHERINE WAS STILL dating Jeff the pilot, but that fall she also began to see a young lawyer named Richard. He was a nice man, pleasant, if unexciting, but the relationship caught Katherine in a vise. She thought she should like him more, and criticized herself for not being able to. That, like everything else, made her wonder what was the matter with her. Katherine, after all, had a way of turning all her feelings into food for the demons.

48

CAROLE'S LITTLE BELLY began to round out a bit and there was nothing but tension between her and Joe Willie. They hadn't paid the doctor the four hundred dollars and the doctor had made it clear that the seventeen-year-old girl couldn't visit him again. She was worried about the pains in her back and the nausea in the morning. She wasn't sure what she should eat and she didn't know if she should even make love. Joe Willie wanted sex more and more, but Carole thought his penis would puncture the womb and hit her baby's head.

"Don't I make it good anymore?" Joe Willie asked her. "Am I letting you down?"

"No, I just don't feel like it."

"Why not? Why not?"

And then sometimes late at night when she did want it, Joe Willie couldn't. He'd drunk too much and he couldn't perform. "You see," Carole complained, "when I want you, you don't want me."

"That's not it," he said. "You know I can never make it when I've had too much to drink."

One minute he was waiting on her with trays and coffee in bed. The next he was yelling and screaming, or withdrawn, almost in a trance.

"What's the matter, Joe Willie?" Carole would ask, and he would ignore her or else yell back, "Shut up, goddamn it!"

"Please, I just want to know what's going on. Can't you tell me?"

Sometimes he stared at her belly. "Why'd you have to go get pregnant?" he asked.

"I didn't 'go get pregnant' and you know it. It just happened."

"Yeah? Well, why? Why me?"

PEOPLE SAID KATHERINE was irritable and restless and Linda Finlay said, "She seemed unstable to me."

Katherine, for her part, sometimes had such loathing and contempt for herself she couldn't stand it. Why was she fingered for that kind of self-hatred and inferiority? she wanted to know. Why had she turned out to have the crooked back and why was she doomed? Everybody had troubles and everybody had doubts, she said to herself and to others, but why were hers worse?

Danny bought Joe Willie an iguana named Rover. The reptile was four feet long and the first time Joe Willie saw it in the store, he petted its prickly head. On the way home in the car, he took the animal out of the cage and held it in his arms as if it were a baby. He cuddled it and kissed its head.

Danny also bought Joe Willie two hamsters. The animals were supposed to be males, so Joe Willie named them Samson and Goliath, after two male winners.

Later, when they turned out to be a male and a female, he changed their names to Samson and Delilah. Delilah, the woman who destroyed Samson by cutting his hair.

50

"JOE WILLIE, HE wanted everything perfect," Carole said. "He wanted dinner the minute he came home from work. And if I wasn't ready he thought I was failing him. If he didn't have 'a good little wife,' he wasn't 'a man.' He couldn't stand it if there was one little thing out of line."

Joe Willie was drinking as much as a quart of Seagrams a day.

"He felt trapped," Danny said. "Trapped in marriage, trapped in the baby coming, trapped in mediocrity. He began to see the whole thing as one more defeat, one more failure, and I don't think he could see his way out of it.

"He was tense and nervous and it showed. One look at him and you knew something was the matter."

His skin was broken out in a rash from the neck down and the veins on his chest and back were striated, red and raw, standing out from his body as if an army of worms had burrowed their way under his skin.

HECTOR WAS A NINE-year-old Puerto Rican boy in Katherine's class at St. Joseph's and in November she brought him south to 72nd Street for the weekend. Katherine told someone she fed him hamburgers and milk and was encouraging him to read. She also said she loved him.

Several days after Hector left she spent some time with a black coke dealer. She told him about the little boy and then she said she didn't know anymore if she would ever have "a normal life."

"What's that?" he asked her.

She said something about a home and children and he looked at her. It was rainy and cold and her raccoon coat was matted and dull. She looked terrible, he remembered. She was an array of bones and scars and her skin was pale. She wasn't as free and loose as she pretended to be, he thought, and just then, he realized, she looked sad.

Winter was coming. The New Jersey sky at night was navy blue and cold. Joe Willie was sitting alone on the couch. The apartment was empty and he was naked except for his undershorts. A brown spiral notebook was on his lap. He had bought it at the New York University bookstore and he used it for things like keeping the running scores for football games and drawing designs for an iguana cage he planned to build.

He opened to a clean sheet and began to write in his neat slanted way. It was the kind of penmanship teachers are proud of and he couldn't always master. This time, though, he did.

"It's hard to put down in words what I have to say," he began, "but it has to be said."

It was to be a letter to Carole, but he never sent it, and she never saw it. "I probably should never have met you or even married you," he wrote. "All I know how to do is wreck people's lives. All I've ever done is hurt people that love me and I'm tired of it."

AT NINE THIRTY ONE night in late November Joe Willie dropped by the New York Council of Alcoholism on East 39th Street. The only person working was Dr. Harold T. Wallace, the director of the center, and "at first," Dr. Wallace said, "he didn't want to talk.

"He was shy, uncertain, but then we sat down and he began to say that he drank too much and used a lot of dope. He said something about one hundred and fifty or two hundred acid trips, back when he was younger. He was worried what this was doing to him. He said he was married and didn't have any money and was having a baby and I got the feeling he was telling me all this so I would reassure him he was going to be all right.

"There was a lost quality about him, something haunting, and I used to think about him afterwards as a perfect example of the people his age we see.

"They're deteriorating rapidly. They have no time, no future. What they need is support and understanding, but they'll never find it. It's too late. They're shut out everywhere. They have nowhere to go."

KATHERINE CALLED HER mother one night before Thanksgiving. She said she was depressed and unhappy and they stayed on the phone for almost half an hour. Mary Cleary tried to learn more about what was bothering her daughter, but the young woman kept saying, "Everything, just everything."

Later Mary Cleary tried to press her again, but this time Katherine acted as if she did not even remember the conversation. "I'm fine, don't worry about me," she said.

"I knew she was very unhappy," Mrs. Cleary said later, "but I didn't know what to do about it."

54

THE MONDAY AFTER Thanksgiving, Joe Willie called Danny at work and asked if they could meet for a drink. At the Club Forty-six Joe Willie told him he was "flipping out." Going crazy. "I just can't stand it anymore," he said. "I'm falling apart."

There, in the shadows of red light bulbs, they talked about Joe Willie's marriage and the baby. Danny felt himself drawn deep into the world inside Joe Willie's head, where, to him, everything was a dead end.

Three days later, Danny got a letter at work from Joe Willie.

Just a line to say something I'd rather say in a note. You see, I'll make it now when I couldn't before because now I have someone to tell my problems to. To be able to get it off my chest is all it'll take to keep me from busting. I never did that before and things were allowed to build up in me and destroy my morals. As long as I have you to lean on and as long as I can unload everything as often as needed, this will all work out. You're a real friend.

55

MARYANN KNEW KATHERINE from the night psychology course they took at Hunter College. In December, she remembered, Katherine was depressed about working so hard.

"Where's it getting me?" she asked once.

Maryann asked her if she was going home for Christmas. Katherine didn't answer. Then she said, "I guess so."

56

JOE WILLIE'S TENSION was acute and the second week in December he quit work.

Then he told Carole she had to go home to Miami. "Why?" she asked.

"I don't want anything to happen to you."

"What do you mean, 'happen to me'? Nothing's going to happen to me."

"I'm flipping out, Carole. I know I am, and I don't want you around. I want you and the baby out of here."

57

ON DECEMBER TWENTIETH, Katherine went to the annual Christmas party at St. Joseph's. She seemed happy, the nuns said later.

58

WHEN CAROLE LEFT, Joe Willie was depressed. "Why don't you go home for Christmas?" Danny said, and gave him the money for the ticket.

It was quiet in Viola Camp during the holidays and Joe Willie sat out on the steps and walked around the block. He didn't talk to anyone or say much about the baby. But he did have presents. With one of Danny's credit cards he had bought five very large suitcases, one for everyone in his family.

The Simpsons were all very surprised by the gifts: They had not, after all, ever traveled and they had no intention of going anywhere.

"You never know," Joe Willie said, "you might just suddenly want to get up and go."

Katherine, in Holyoke for Christmas, returned to New York on the twenty-eighth. No one who saw her during the next few days noticed anything unusual. She was the same: halfway up and halfway down. As the New Year approached, she told someone she hoped 1973 would be better.

ON DECEMBER THIRTY-FIRST, Joe Willie flew back to New York. Danny met him at the airport and they drove into the city by cab. It was late and Joe Willie said he wanted to go to Times Square to watch the New Year come in.

There were hundreds of thousands of people in Times Square and Danny was unnerved by it. "It was like a crowd that's about to riot. It was almost out of control and I wanted to get out of there, but not Joe Willie. He got into it. People were pushing and he was pushing harder. He was very aggressive and hostile. It turned him on. I'd never seen him like that. He was almost a different person."

Suddenly, on 44th and Broadway, they saw a group of teenagers harassing a young woman. They were hitting her, trying to grab her breasts, drunkenly jostling her, and she was crying. Her date was cowering in the background. The woman kept calling his name but he didn't move to help her. He was paralyzed and the kids kept twisting her breasts, touching her stomach and hair.

It all happened in seconds, and suddenly, twenty-six hours before the murder, Joe Willie leapt at the kids like a tiger, "ferocious and angry," Danny said.

He grabbed the woman in his arms. He fought off the attackers. He kicked and shoved at them, and all the time she was crying on his neck. "Don't worry," he kept saying, "don't worry," soothing, strong.

Then suddenly the scene was over. The kids ran away. The date came back to retrieve the girl. He took her by the arm, and they disappeared.

Joe Willie was alone. "Damn it," he said angrily to Danny. "I should have made a pass at her."

KATHERINE SPENT NEW Year's Eve alone at home. She cooked spaghetti and read *Deliverance*.

The next day, the day of the murder, she lay in bed and went on reading. She passed the homosexual rape scene and had almost finished the book when she put it down and got dressed to go outside.

61

THAT SAME DAY, THE day of the murder, Danny woke up early. "I remember lying there thinking, 'This is going to be a terrific day, a terrific year,'" he said.

Joe Willie slept until four in the afternoon and that night they walked across 72nd Street, past Broadway to Columbus Avenue, to a restaurant for dinner. It was bitter cold.

"I don't remember our conversation at dinner," Danny said. "It was about this and that, and then we left. We started walking down 72nd toward West End. We had almost turned the corner toward home when Joe Willie said, 'Let's stop and have a drink.' We'd never been in Tweed's before."

They pushed against the old wooden door and, leaving behind the cold bitter wind in the street, they went inside.

62

THERE AMIDST THE heat and the smoke, beneath the dangling spider plants, Katherine was sitting alone at the bar drinking Johnny Walker Red. Joe Willie and Danny

edged their way past her through the crowd and found a
spot by the bar near the cash register.

Someone beside them was talking about the football
game. Jack Pawling, behind the bar, was tired from the
night before. Danny was bored. Joe Willie was edgy. Katherine ordered another drink, and about ten o'clock Joe
Willie started to talk to a man named Rafe seated alongside him. Steve Levine looked at the bar over his shoulder
and noticed Rafe talking to someone, but he did not see
Joe Willie or Danny. Instead he saw Katherine in the shadows. She looked depressed and he went over to cheer her
up. They talked about a lot of things, even Freddie Watson.

"Hey, look, Joe Willie, I'm pushing off," Danny said. "I
want to start the New Year right."

"Okay. I'll stay, have a couple more, and see you later."

Danny tied the scarf around his neck, and gave a last
look at Joe Willie standing there at the bar, his blue shirt
open at the neck. He wished Joe Willie would leave; he'd
already had too much to drink.

Steve drifted away from Katherine. She was alone again.
She pushed the hair out of her eyes and looked out across
the room. There were a lot of faces that were familiar, and
some that were not. Rafe drew the pictures of Mickey
Mouse and then Donald Duck, and Joe Willie asked for
another drink. On the jukebox Leonard Cohen was singing the sad tale of Suzanne and the River and Our Lady
of the Harbor.

Katherine moved out into the room; she talked to
friends and then she went back to the bar. She got a drink
and chatted with Pawling and then after a while he introduced her to the man drinking Seagrams.

"What'd you say your name was?" he asked Joe Willie.
"Charlie Smith."

"That's right," he said. "Charlie Smith, meet Katherine Cleary."

She had noticed him before. He was a tall man and his face was smooth from the eyes down to the place where the shadows of his whiskers began. His eyes were blue and sometimes they looked out straight and strong, and other times he had a way of bending his head, almost like a bird, and then his eyes looked hooded, withdrawn and shy.

Now she was looking him right in the face and she smiled. "Hi," she said with warmth. And he looked back at her. "Hi," he said.

From this point on nothing is known about what Joe Willie said or what Katherine said or what either one of them thought or wanted or felt or saw. It is known, of course, about what they did and where they went and something is known about what happened in the room across the street, but nothing is known about all the little things that tell you why it happened. There is no way of knowing, for example, if Katherine looked at this man and the tilt of his head and the leather on his boots and saw something that could have been a warning to her. There is no way of knowing how the yearning and the gnawing in her heart influenced her that night.

But if you know Katherine and you know Joe Willie and you remember their gentle kindness and fine smiles and good looks, then you may imagine that quite possibly they liked each other a lot at first. That is what most people who saw them then surmised, and if you think about that, their talking and their meeting might well have gone like this:

Joe Willie looked down at Katherine. Her thick red hair shined and curled around her face. Her skin was soft, light, and a smile began to move in across her face as he watched her. "Lady," he said, gazing at her, "I grew up as a kid down in Texas and there was this woman ran a store out back in the fields and I swear, you're the first person I've ever seen since had more freckles 'an her." He paused. "Lady," he added, "you have one nice set of freckles."

His voice was round and rolling and strong and Katherine started to laugh. "I don't know whether to believe you or not," she said.

"About what? The nice set of freckles?"

"No, no." She was smiling, happy. "About Texas, the store in the fields."

"What about it?" He looked happy.

"Is that true?"

"Of course."

"The woman, the store, and all?"

"Of course," he nodded. "But I spent most of my life in Chicago. I'm a city person."

"Me, too, but I grew up in the country. Not country like you, but New Jersey country."

"All's the same in one way," he said. "If you got that touch of the country in you somewhere, it's there and it stays."

She nodded. She thought so, too, she said.

He bought the next round of drinks and he said he was in town looking for a job. She asked, what'd he do, and he said, too much traveling, and didn't really answer.

Then he rolled out the pictures Rafe had done to show her. "See these?" he said.

She looked. "Nice."

"Pretty good, no?"

She nodded.

"Only cost me six dollars apiece," he said proudly.

"Six dollars!" she said aghast. She looked at him. "You must still be from the country," she said. Her voice had changed. It was hard, driven with a hammer. "You got took, mister."

"How so?" His voice changed, too. He was angry.

"Rafe never charged that much in his life. He took you for a sucker."

Joe Willie almost responded to that but, instead, he turned off in another direction and said, "Maybe not. Depends, of course, on how much money a fellow's got. That might look like 'took' to folks like you," he said, slow, easy, "but it might look like pure generosity and kindness to folks like me with plenty of bucks."

He smiled. There had been no collision. One boat had swerved at the last minute.

Katherine looked at him and some part of her went back on course, too. She noticed his leather jacket on the counter. It was expensive.

Hey, she said, did he want to put money in the jukebox. There were some good songs. And she jumped off the stool. "Come on," she said, and headed off into the crowd ahead of him.

He didn't move, but turned his head to look after her. She was limping. He watched the uneven cadence of her walk and remembered a young woman named Annie who was a friend of Danny's. She'd had polio as a child and walked with a limp. Joe Willie had often told Danny she was one of the nicest people he knew, with "one of the best smiles in the world." This Katherine had a good smile, too, he thought, and then he picked up his jacket and his drawings and followed her.

She was up against the jukebox. It was crowded. Lots of folks pressed in everywhere and he pressed up against her and they played songs. She talked about her school and after a while, as she talked on, Joe Willie got restless, even bored, and he said to her, Lady, he was thinking of moving on.

And she said the night was young. Why didn't he stick around? She was thinking that she liked talking to him, liked the way he listened and maybe, when he got his job in New York . . .

He said the night wasn't as young as she thought.

But before he could leave, a group of people said why didn't everybody move across the street to the Hatch?

Katherine said great, let's go. She rounded up some friends. Joe Willie put on his coat, took his drawings, and went, too.

Outside the cold was bitter, the wind hard, and Joe Willie pulled his collar up around his neck. In the Copper Hatch he told the bartender he wanted "Chablis," or, as he pronounced it, "Chablisss," and Katherine laughed.

"You must still be in the sticks."

He looked confused.

"Chab-lee," she told him, enunciating in an arch, exaggerated way. "Chab-lee."

"Yes, ma'am, teacher," he said, good-natured, but sarcastic and derisive.

And then he and Katherine talked. They talked and talked this time and it was rather nice between them. It was getting late and around them people were leaving, the bartender was cleaning up for the night. At some point Joe Willie and Katherine got up, too.

They went next door to Katherine's building and took the elevator up to the seventh floor. Katherine unlocked Apartment Seven-One-Five and they went inside.

"IT WAS A MESS," Joe Willie told Danny later. "It looked like it hadn't been cleaned in weeks."

Clothes were all over the floor. A box of sugar had spilled on the floor. The sofa bed was unmade, opened out into the middle of the room, and there were dirty dishes in the kitchen. Spaghetti sauce had dribbled down the front of the stove, and orange juice had hardened on the floor.

The twenty-three-year-old man looked around with the eyes of someone who had always lived in a spotless house and liked it that way. His sense of the woman shifted and took on an element of disgust.

Katherine got some grass from a tin on the windowsill. Joe Willie tried to roll a joint, but he'd drunk too much and he couldn't do it. His fingers slipped.

"I'll do it," Katherine said, taking the papers. She acted irritated, as if he'd done something wrong and he felt it.

She didn't talk much. They leaned back against the pillows on the bed and smoked in silence.

Then after a while he reached over to touch her. Her breasts were little and he felt them. Picking up a book of matches she lit the red candles by the bed and turned out the light. He began to unbutton her blouse and feel her skin. She stood up to take off her pants and turned then to hide the angle of her back. She stepped out of her underpants and dropped them on the floor beside the bed. He undressed, too, took off his blue plaid shorts, and lay down alongside her.

Time passed.

Nobody knows what happened. Maybe they made love then and Joe Willie, who hadn't been inside a woman for a while, came deep in her body. Maybe Katherine, too, felt what she wanted to there between her legs and it was good. But maybe none of this happened. At least then. Or, maybe Joe Willie made fun of her, or, maybe she made fun of him. Maybe he was the one who got nasty first, or, maybe she was. Maybe Joe Willie started the awful fight, or, maybe she started it.

Nobody knows. And the only versions left are Joe Willie's, and this is one version:

> "First we balled." And then, finished, he said, they were lying on the wrinkled sheets when "she went nuts and started pushing me physically to hurry and get dressed and leave. She was very nasty, a complete reversal of a few moments before. I have problems with my mines [sic] and I often flip out, not knowing whether walls, people, etcetera, are real. I hear things, I think sometimes I can even fly.
> "Well, she started shoving me and I blew up, not mad,

I wasn't mad or anything, just very cold and hurt. I grabbed her and held her on the bed and tried to talk to her, to get a reason for her sudden rejection of me. She started saying kill me, kill me, please. I had no intention of killing anyone when I went there. Then she said I was crazy, she could see it. She tried to get up so I grabbed her around the throat and started choking her. I choked her for a long time but when I flip out I can't see too well and I thought she was still alive. I then took her pants, which were on the floor next to the bed, and choked her with them for a long while. I hit her a few more times and then I went to the kitchen and got a paring knife and I stabbed her several times, once hitting the jugular vein."

A torrent of blood spurted up out of her neck. It splashed in his face and made a huge, grotesque picture on the wall behind the bed. Blood was pouring from her body It spilled out over Joe Willie's stomach and along his arms and legs. He went over to the windowsill and got a large red candle. "I stuffed it in her vagina," he said, "and it broke off in my hand."

Then he got to his feet. He stood in the middle of the room by the bed; his arms were hanging out at his sides, and his penis was large and full. The end was big, round, the rest of it long and thick. He stood there breathing and breathing. He looked back at the schoolteacher. Her eyes were open, staring in terror, her body spewing out blood.

He looked at her more. Then he reached out and laid his fingertips tenderly on her eyelids. He moved them slightly and brought the open, frightened eyes to a close. "She didn't look good that way," he said later, "and I didn't want her watching me."

Then, his body covered with her blood, he went to the bathroom and turned on the shower. He washed himself, and the water flowed red down the drain. It was three thirty. He went back into the room and, with the faucet still running behind him, he picked up her turquoise blue bathrobe. He laid it across the wounds of the body. He said he thought "she looked better that way."

Then he went around the apartment, turning over chairs and emptying out drawers. He took her wallet and some money, and the white lace slip, and as he was leaving he picked up the large white statue of Katherine Cleary and, in one last surge of anger, he threw it hard at her face. "There's a lot I don't remember," he said, in ending, "and I just walked around all night."

That's the story Joe Willie told the police and it is probably mostly true. He gave it to them first in words and then he wrote it down on paper. He did not mention, however, that at some point he bent over her body and chewed fiercely on her breasts, leaving ragged blue cuts and marks all over the little white bosoms.

Joe Willie Simpson gave Carole Musty and Danny Murray, and a court-appointed lawyer he liked, another version of what had happened. This is story number two, and it is probably mostly true too:

They went up to her apartment, he said, and they began to smoke dope. They leaned against the pillows on the sofa bed, and after a while Katherine lit the candles, and he started to touch her little breasts, and she reached in between his legs to caress his body. Then they got undressed and, lying down again, her hands moved down his belly past the blond hair, and found his penis. She rubbed over it and it rolled round, soft, like a deflated balloon, and he, licking her neck, whispered, "Sorry, sorry," he'd had too much to drink. But she felt it more, rubbed and pulled but it didn't grow or swell or turn hard and then, as sure as spit and fire, the atmosphere began to change.

She got angry, mean, Joe Willie said, and before he knew it, she was hysterical, screeching at him to get dressed and hurry up and leave and she said, "You're just like all the rest, you suck," and he yelled at her, "Bitch, cunt," and she said, "Yah?" taunting, "Get me, get me," and he blew up. He wasn't mad or anything, he just got cold, hurt. It hurt him what she said, and she said, "Yah! My brothers'll get you," and he grabbed her, held her on the bed and squeezed her and she squirmed and moaned beneath him and mumbled, "Kill me, kill me, please." And then she began to try to push him off and to fight him back, but he had her by the throat and he choked her tight with his hands and then he leaned over and grabbed her underpants from the floor. He wound them around her neck and pulled in each direction. Then he got the knife and he came back to the bed and sprawled over her body and stabbed her again and again, eighteen times in the neck and belly. . . .

That's the story Joe Willie Simpson gave his wife, his best friend, and his lawyer. The main thing that was different between what he told them and what he told the police was that here he had been impotent. That's what started everything off, he said—but didn't tell the police—he had failed as a man.

And it's probably mostly true.

But what Joe Willie never explained in his story to Carole or Danny or the lawyer was how he left the white seminal fluid the autopsy found.

There was yet a third story, but Joe Willie didn't tell it to anyone except later, his lawyer. One other person, the jail psychiatrist, didn't hear it—and Joe Willie never told him—but when he was talking with Joe Willie and trying to figure out what had happened up there in that apartment, he decided something on his own and that turned out to be the same thing as story number three. This story begins after the murder, after Joe Willie had been unable to fuck her. It picks up where the second story ended, when Katherine Cleary was lying on her back, dead and bleeding:

> After Joe Willie had yelled and screamed and punched her and choked her and stabbed her and stabbed her and stabbed her and stabbed her, then he did what he'd been unable to do before. His penis was full and large and heavy with all the anger and fury and power that had been building and building in him since he walked the fields and roamed the country and cuddled the iguana and finally now it erupted out in rage against this woman and now triumphant, he rode that dead woman like a horse, he rode her and rode her with his penis hard and fast in the place inside that was still warm.

64

BACK ON 69th STREET Danny Murray woke up. It was about three thirty in the morning and Joe Willie still hadn't come home. "I'd never worried about this before, but that night I went out looking for him. I went back to Tweed's but it was closed. When I came home he was sitting on the couch in his undershorts. I pretended to be mad. 'Where in hell have you been?' I said.

" 'Sit down. I want to tell you something.'

"He told me right away. He was in a daze. I'd never seen

him like that before. He was staring straight ahead at the wall and talking not to me but to the wall. He was in a state of talking to the world and to nobody, as if he was trying to tell himself it was true. He kept saying, 'I'm glad it wasn't anybody I knew.'

"I sat there and listened. I didn't know what to think or how to react. I just kept wanting to make it all stop. Not to be. What had happened? Who was this schoolteacher? What had she done to all our lives? Joe Willie didn't talk about her or describe her then. He just said that she insulted him and it tore him up and suddenly he flipped out. He couldn't take it anymore. He said she said, 'Kill me, kill me I dare you to kill me If you do, my brothers will get you for it.' I can't imagine a girl saying that, but I believe it. He had no right to take a life, but sometimes you can start something and not know when to stop.

"I didn't know if he was telling the truth. The killing made no sense. If he'd come home and said, 'I met a guy and he paid me three thousand dollars to kill a girl and I did it,' I would have believed him. There would be a reason. This way, there was no reason."

Finally about six o'clock in the morning Joe Willie got up and went to the bedroom to go to sleep. Danny brought him a glass of water and a sedative. Joe Willie swallowed the pill and handed the glass back to Danny.

Then he said, "If you call the police, Danny, be gentle, because you know I don't wake up very easily. I sleep soundly, so be gentle."

Danny did not call the police.

Joe Willie woke up that afternoon about three and after a brief discussion they decided he should get out of town.

Danny gave him some money. He flew to Miami and checked into the Sunnyside Hotel. He slept all night and most of Wednesday. On New Year's night he had broken bones and ripped flesh, severed muscles, veins, ligaments, and organs, and instead of knowing that was why his body ached like hell, he thought he was getting a cold.

He went out to buy aspirins, came back and slept some more.

On Wednesday night he got up and went out again. He picked up a prostitute, went back to her place, fucked her, and left. That was something he hadn't done in years. He didn't like hookers. The way he put it, they degraded the finest thing on earth: Woman.

BACK IN NEW YORK Danny Murray was looking for stories in the newspapers, but there were none. He was frantic about Joe Willie. About two thirty Thursday morning Joe Willie called and said he felt "terrible, terrible."

"He was down, mentally and physically," Danny remembered, "and he said he needed some sort of relief. He said he'd gone out and picked up some girl and that it hadn't helped. That scared me. I didn't know if he'd do it again. Kill, I mean. I kept remembering him saying, 'Thank God it was somebody I didn't know.' He never did say anything about the schoolteacher and I didn't know what state he was in. All he said was he thought he was getting a cold. I didn't know what he might do next. He said he was going to call Carole and I didn't know if I should call her and warn her or what."

He should have been worried about himself. The little schoolteacher was coming a whole lot closer to him than he knew.

THURSDAY THERE WERE two developments in the case. First, the murder, after a one-day delay, finally turned up in the police "Unusuals Report" and reached the reporters. It would be all over the front pages the next morning. And, second, for the first time now the police began to think of Charlie Smith as something more than just another figure who'd been in Tweed's New Year's night. The pictures of Mickey Mouse and Donald Duck in the apartment had established a definite connection between him and the deceased.

Freddie Watson, however, was still the prime suspect. Watson had a motive, and Smith, as far as they knew, had none. In addition, the police still hadn't been able to locate Watson, to find out where he was on January first. He wasn't at any of his usual hangouts and some police were beginning to wonder if he'd skipped.

Back on 72nd Street, however, Cooley and McBride

were still following the trail of Charlie Smith and his friend or brother. So far they were having trouble finding anyone who remembered Smith. Instead, people said they thought they remembered the tall thin man with him.

Cooley and McBride were headed back to Tweed's again. Across the street at Two-Five-Three, reporters and photographers, who had just found out about the murder, were backed up ten-deep on the sidewalk trying to get inside. The super and a bunch of patrolmen were keeping them out.

Inside the bar Steve Levine was cleaning up from the night before.

"What'd he look like?" they asked him.

"I told you before," Steve said. "I didn't get a look at him. I only remember the other guy. He was tall, blond, balding maybe; I can't tell you much more than that."

Pawling, however, thought that Charlie Smith had been tall and blond and the other dark with short hair. Rafe had said the same thing. "They musta been brothers," he said. "They looked alike."

Some at Tweed's who remembered the two men said they were both blond, others said they were both dark, some remembered glasses, some didn't, and there was no consensus on the color of their eyes, their ages, or their clothes. The only thing they agreed upon was that they all felt more definite about the friend.

"God damn," said Cooley. "Hard to tell which of these guys is which."

Only one woman had a strong recollection. She had seen Charlie Smith in the Copper Hatch. "He was big in the shoulders, blond," she said, "and he held his head to the left. He had on a leather jacket. He was well dressed."

"You mean the Park Avenue type?"

"No, I mean he wasn't down and out, creepy. He wasn't a freak. There was something nice about him. I don't know, really," she interjected. "It's just an impression."

"That's okay. Keep going."

"He was nice. I liked him. She was teasing him about being a hick. He didn't like it."

"Did they have a fight?"

"No. He just seemed to get defensive. I didn't hear the conversation or anything. I just heard her laugh loud and I looked. That's what I saw."

"Was he her date?"

"I don't know 'date.' But they were together."

"What about the drawings?"

"I didn't see any."

"He had a couple of drawings, Mickey Mouse and Donald Duck."

"I don't know. He was carrying something under his arm. Some papers or books. I don't know what it was."

One man remembered the papers. They were rolled up, he said, round, like a calendar, and the guy carried them in his hand.

"Did they leave together?" McBride asked.

"I would think they could have, but I didn't see it."

The detectives found someone else, though, who had seen Katherine go home. It was about two, two thirty, he said, and she was with someone.

"Who?" asked McBride.

"No idea."

"Never saw him before?"

"I don't know, because I didn't even see his face."
"What was he wearing?"
"I don't know."
"A leather jacket?"
"I don't know."

JOE WILLIE CALLED Carole that Thursday afternoon and told her to take a cab to the hotel. She arrived in a white sundress that showed her shoulders, her breasts, and the shape of her belly. Joe Willie met her on the street and took her back to his room.

"He was tremendously happy to see me and vice versa," Carole said. "I hadn't seen him in a week and I missed him a lot. We talked and talked and it was wonderful. We lay on the bed and held each other for a long time. He was very quiet, very soft and very gentle. He was different than I'd ever seen him and I wanted him to hold me in his arms forever. Then he started undressing me and kissing me and he got up and went to the bathroom to shave and he undressed and I saw all the scratches. I asked him where they came from and he said he had a fight in a bar with some guy because he sat down with the guy's chick and the guy got all upset and Joe Willie finally punched him and he went through the window and Joe Willie had to run. I believed him. Then he laid back down on the bed and we started to make love. And he was so kind and gentle and he rubbed my belly and felt the baby kicking. It was nice and we made love and I felt it everywhere. It was the only time during the whole time I was pregnant I enjoyed sex with him. Maybe it was because it was going to be the last time and some part of me knew it.''

DANNY CALLED JOE Willie and asked him to speak to Carole. He talked to her long enough to determine that Joe Willie had done nothing to frighten her.

ON FRIDAY IT WAS in the papers:

"SAVAGE CRIME OF PASSION: YOUNG TEACHER SLAIN ON WEST SIDE," blared four-inch-tall headlines on the front page of the *Daily News*.

"TEACHER, 28, SLAIN IN HER APARTMENT ON THE WEST SIDE," said the *New York Times* on the top half of page one.

Danny bought both papers and read the *Times* first quickly.

A twenty-eight-year-old teacher of deaf children was found knifed to death in the efficiency apartment on West 72nd Street to which she had moved because she was impressed with the comparative security of the building and the street.

According to a police spokesman, the body of Katherine Cleary was discovered after officials of the St. Joseph's School for the Deaf in the Bronx became alarmed when Miss Cleary failed to return to her class after the Christmas recess. A colleague of Miss Cleary's from the school went to the building, which is near West End Avenue, and had the superintendent open the door to her two-room apartment on the seventh floor.

Detectives said that Miss Cleary's body had been found on a sofa and that she had been repeatedly stabbed. A hollow sculptured bust of a woman had been placed on her face, they said. An autopsy by a medical examiner showed that Miss Cleary had been raped and that she had been stabbed fourteen times.

The examiner said there were bruises on her face.

Detectives from the Fourth Division homicide and assault team said yesterday that they had no leads in their investigation.

"No leads," Danny thought. "No leads. Was it true?"

The rest of the story went on for almost three columns, and contained no reference to Joe Willie or any suspect. Instead it mentioned the schoolteacher once had polio, was well liked throughout the neighborhood and "was very dedicated to her work." There was a picture. It showed a very pretty woman with sunglasses and long full hair.

He went on to the *Daily News.*

An attractive young teacher who had dedicated her life to helping the handicapped was found naked, apparently raped, stabbed twenty times and brutally bludgeoned with a statuette of herself in her small West Side apartment, police disclosed yesterday.

The victim, red-haired Katherine Cleary, twenty-eight-year-old daughter of a New Jersey executive, was found sprawled on a convertible bed in her studio apartment at 253 West 72nd Street between Broadway and West End Avenue.

Apparently after stabbing the slim Katherine in the neck and abdomen, the killer had picked up the bust—a likeness of Katherine—and smashed her full in the face with it. He also had punched her face.

The story went on to another page and Danny skipped to a large feature story: "SHE HEARD PLEAS OF THE DEAF." The reporter had apparently gotten into the apartment. The story began:

The title of the book on the convertible bed yesterday was "Deliverance," a popular tale of violence and sudden death.

But there had been no deliverance for its owner, teacher Katherine Cleary, twenty-eight, who was stabbed and bludgeoned to death in her gloomy, cramped studio apartment on West 72nd Street.

Her body lay on the scrambled bedding and blood was splattered on the walls like some morbid abstract painting.

The killer had slipped out unnoticed. There was nothing left to tell the story of Katherine Cleary but her naked body, her books, which added a pathetic dash of color to the dimly lit apartment, her cheap furniture and her pet cat.

Two other books lying near the bed gave mute testimony

to Katherine's interests—"Speech and Hearing Science" and "Talk to the Deaf."

The apartment, on the seventh floor, faces a door to the stairwell. Fingerprint powder on the door illustrated detectives' theory that an intruder had climbed the stairs, knocked on the first door he saw, Katherine's, and somehow persuaded her to open it.

Then, while the rest of the city celebrated the holidays, he had done his murderous work and fled.

70

FRIDAY AFTERNOON Frank and Don Cleary drove in to clean up the apartment. They gave Missy, the cat, away and packed their sister's belongings in carton boxes.

"She was such a weak little thing," Frank told a friend afterward. "She tried hard to be strong, but she just never made it."

71

AT THE SAME TIME, Danny went out to buy the *New York Post,* the afternoon paper, and what he read frightened him all the way down to the soles of his feet.

Stories about the upcoming Truman memorial service in Washington, the strike on the Long Island Railroad, and a threatened shutdown of the city subway system were all inside.

The large cover headline read: "SIFT 2 ANGLES IN SLAYING OF TEACHER." It was the only story on the whole front page and it began:

> The investigation of the murder of Katherine Cleary, attractive twenty-eight-year-old teacher of deaf children found slain in her West Side apartment, appeared to be focused on two areas:
>
> Finding the man with whom she had been seen in neighborhood bars the night before her death.

Danny was alarmed. He read the paragraph over again and then continued.

> Checking the whereabouts at the time of her death of a man once arrested for striking her, reportedly because she spurned his advances.
>
> Both of those leads were being pursued on the theory that the slain woman probably knew her killer.
>
> Although offering few details, police said today that they had questioned a number of Miss Cleary's acquaintances who reported seeing her Monday night with a man who so far remains unidentified. At the same time detectives indicated interest in the movements that same night of the man arrested last May for hitting her—though they stressed that at this time there is no evidence implicating him in the death.
>
> "We don't have any suspects yet," said Lt. Michael Kraft, commander of the Fourth District Homicide Squad, "but there are things we're pursuing."

That night Joe Willie called Danny from a pay phone and asked him if "the radio" had said anything about "the event."

Danny said yes and read him the stories.

Joe Willie listened quietly and was not upset. Afterward he expressed no remorse or any curiosity about the woman's life as it was revealed in the papers. He was only concerned about what, if anything, could connect him with the man the paper said people saw with Katherine that night.

They talked about that and finally reached the conclusion Joe Willie was safe. He'd left no fingerprints; no one had seen him do it; and even, they agreed, if people did remember him, they had no idea who he was. There was no way the police could trace him.

As it turned out, they were almost right. There was just one thing neither Joe Willie nor Danny calculated, and Danny, for one, would remember that forever.

They agreed to talk the next day and said good night.

Saturday, however, brought even more alarming information. The *New York Times* made only a passing reference to police interest in the man who had assaulted the teacher once before. Instead the paper quoted a source saying now the police unofficially had a "definite suspect." It was the same man referred to in the newspaper the day before, the man people saw with her in the neighborhood the night she died.

The man described as young and white, but as yet unidentified by name, apparently frequented the same few bars Miss Cleary did, sometimes with her, sometimes with a man the police said was his brother.

Until this man is cleared, a source said, he is "a suspect."

The story also noted that earlier reports that the woman had been raped were untrue, and quoted the deputy chief medical examiner. He said:

There was none of the external or internal signs of force or brutality that would indicate she had objected to sexual intercourse.

Danny called Joe Willie and read him this article. Joe Willie didn't respond. He didn't say anything. Then after a while, he said, "I can't take this hotel anymore."

It was getting to him, he went on, and he wanted to go home. Danny said he didn't think that was such a good idea, but it would probably be all right for him to go to his brother Fred's in Springfield.

They talked for a while and Danny listened to the sound of Joe Willie's voice. It was a monotone. Slow. Stagnant. Lifeless.

Danny wondered what was going to happen. He knew it wouldn't be good. But he didn't know it would be the thing it turned out to be.

Afterward he wired Joe Willie money for the ticket to Illinois and sometime that day Joe Willie left Miami.

ON SATURDAY THERE was a funeral service for Katherine Cleary at St. Ann's Roman Catholic Church, about a mile from the house in Holyoke. About two hundred and fifty people attended. It was a cold winter day.

The solemn requiem mass was celebrated by six priests. These included two priests affiliated with St. Joseph's School for the Deaf, and Katherine's first cousin, the Rev. Frank McGee, assistant pastor at St. Mary's Roman Catholic Church in Queens.

Vincent and Mary and Frank and Don were there and Father McGee said of his cousin: "She possessed a loving acceptance of herself and other people—that lovingness that children could detect and respond to. She was a sincere girl who tried in such a few years to open our lives and the lives of others. And now, in her death, she tells us how to be open and to try to understand His plan, even when it seems to be so contradictory that the innocent must suffer."

Louie McBride, Tom Cooley and Michael Kraft attended the funeral. They drove out early from New York to be on hand to watch the crowd arrive—on the chance the murderer had decided to come, too. They didn't know who they were looking for.

Maybe a man who was tall or thin or dark or blond or bald or wore glasses.

NOW IT WAS SUNDAY, January seventh.

It was going to be the biggest day in Danny Murray's life. But it started out slow, quiet.

Sundays had never been important to Danny, largely because, until he met Joe Willie, he was the kind of person who was always busy. When he wasn't working, he was thinking about working or working overtime or meeting friends or going to the theater. Sometimes he did let the time spill over and seep out into the day like a pool of fallen water spreading across an incline, but only when he was depressed. Only when all the things that circulated slowly, stealthily, menacingly, around his life closed in on him and bayed and howled up near like wild dogs.

But all this had changed when Joe Willie came into his life. He was happier than he'd ever been before. He was loved. He was needed. He was useful. He was getting to be a father and a friend and a lover all at once, and, also, for the first time, he had learned about having fun. Not just keeping busy.

"What are we gonna do to have some fun?" Joe Willie would say. He'd say it all the time, especially on Sundays. "What are we gonna do to have some fun?" And he always had ideas. Uncanny things. Going to Coney Island and riding the roller coaster. Taking the Staten Island Ferry. Going to Nathan's for a hot dog. And lying in bed Sunday, January seventh, Danny was thinking about this.

Joe Willie would love this day. The sky was blue. It was cold. Joe Willie would look out the window and across the hills and in no time at all he'd have a plan.

But, God, where was he today? In Springfield, roached up somewhere with his brother?

Fuck, what a mess.

Danny got up and went out to buy the papers. He plunked the quarters down on the newsstand, picked up the pounds of material, saw there was nothing on the front pages and headed home.

Back on the thirty-second floor, he opened the *Times* and without warning the schoolteacher reached out and grabbed his life by the throat and squeezed.

He saw the picture first. Sketch. White male. Short hair. Unrecognizable.

Then the headline. Large type, eight columns across top of page.

"POLICE ISSUE A SKETCH OF WITNESS THEY HOPE WILL IDENTIFY KILLER OF TEACHER IN WEST SIDE APARTMENT."

Police detectives investigating last week's knife slaying of twenty-eight-year-old Katherine Cleary in her West Side apartment said yesterday that they were searching for a witness who might be able to identify her killer.

The witness himself has not yet been identified but a description of him and a composite sketch were released by Deputy Inspector William Silvano of the Manhattan Borough detectives in command in a late afternoon news conference at the 20th Precinct on 82nd Street.

Inspector Silvano said the witness "may be able to help us locate and identify" the victim's last known companion, a young man who was seen with her in neighborhood bars Monday night.

Danny skipped over the article.

> . . . Inspector . . . urged him to make himself known to the police . . .
>
> Urged . . . public to provide information on his identity . . . or whereabouts . . . special telephone number . . . white man, twenty-eight to thirty-two years old, six feet tall, weighing one hundred and sixty-five pounds, fair complexion, short cropped light brown hair . . . Lt. Michael Kraft . . . described the witness as "very important" . . . said . . . inquiry . . . had reached "sensitive stage" . . .

Danny had been frightened all along about how this whole thing was going to turn out.

Now, for the first time, he was frightened for himself.

BACK AT THE 20th Precinct there had been a lot of disagreement about releasing the sketch. The old story about how the sketch only appears when the leads have dried up was true. It was generally viewed as a last-ditch effort in the case—short of time and a miracle—but a number of officers still strenuously opposed the move on the ground it was too soon.

This'll tip the guy's hand and he'll skip, they argued. He'll know we're looking for him and keep low. Both of them, for that matter, will know.

Furthermore, they argued, the sketch had gotta be lousy—the witnesses were just too vague—and no one was ever gonna recognize anybody on the basis of that.

But there was the other point of view, too, and it won. The police didn't have anything more to go on. Every corner trash basket for fifteen blocks had been examined, every apartment and every store canvassed, every friend interviewed, every lead followed. The labs had come up with nothing and even Freddie Watson, it turned out, had a lock-tight alibi. And they had no idea who in hell Charlie Smith and his brother were.

And who knows, they argued, putting the sketch out might flush something up.

DANNY CALLED HIS lawyer. He told him about the picture.

They talked on the phone just long enough for the lawyer to catch the urgency and he told Danny to come right over.

They sat in the living room. The two men were personal friends and Danny told him everything and Frank Mil-

stadt, one of the city's leading attorneys, said theoretically
he could face four possible criminal charges.

They were felony indictments for obstruction of justice,
destruction of evidence, being an accessory to a crime, or
even as an accomplice to the crime itself. The crime, of
course, was murder one.

He had three basic options: (1) run, (2) do nothing
and cross his fingers and wait, or (3) go to the authorities.

He, Milstadt, recommended the last.

They circled that subject, option number three, like
elephants on thin ice, but it boiled down to one hard ball
of wax and they both knew it. Now Danny and Joe Willie
were both in trouble.

And either Joe Willie or Danny or both were gonna get
it.

If you let me go, I'll give you Joe Willie. If you let me
go, I'll give you Joe Willie.

"Do I have to do it?" Danny asked.

"No."

"Why can't I wait and see what happens?"

"You can. But if you wait and see what happens, and
then you get caught, or Joe Willie gets caught, then it's a
whole new ball game."

"Why?"

"Then it's too late. Then you have nothing they need
and there's nothing they owe you. This way they owe
you."

76

FRANK MILSTADT CALLED Assistant District Attorney
William Taylor, chief of homicide in the Manhattan district attorney's office, at home. They, too, were friends
and Milstadt said he had a client who had pertinent information about the murder of Katherine Cleary.

Who was he? Taylor asked.

Milstadt didn't answer but he said, if the state would
give his client immunity for any role he might have played
in the crime, the client would be willing to discuss it with
the authorities.

Taylor listened. Milstadt had mentioned no names or
details.

"Can you give me any idea who this fellow is or what
he's got?" Taylor asked.

Milstadt didn't answer.

"Can he give us the murderer?" Taylor asked. It was the
key question.

Milstadt didn't answer.

Taylor then made an appointment with Milstadt to discuss the matter in person at two o'clock the next afternoon. He knew Milstadt was too good to be calling about
penny ante stuff.

Then Taylor called the Fourth Division Homicide
Squad to find out what was going on. So far there was no

case, no charge, no defendant, and the unsolved murder of Katherine Cleary was only a police matter. It had nothing to do with the D.A.'s office.

He talked to Kraft, an old friend, and heard the story of the two men in the bar, Rafe, the drawings, the murder, the witnesses, and the sketch. Mostly, though, they talked about the fact that there was no evidence and this Charlie fellow, whoever he was, might be as guilty as Attila the Hun, but they couldn't prove it. Then Taylor told him about Milstadt and they wondered what Milstadt had.

If he had the friend, he had a lot.

DANNY MURRAY WALKED home from Milstadt's. The lawyer was going to call Taylor and if things worked out, he said, the next step was a meeting in the district attorney's office to set the ground rules. After that it was Danny's turn.

The thirty-nine-year-old man who'd grown up alongside a grain elevator walked the city streets. His head was low, a buffer to the wind. It was cold and clear and bright, but no part of him wanted to lift his face to the light or feel his head in the sky. He wanted to crawl underground.

He hadn't talked to Joe Willie since yesterday and he wouldn't call him tonight. He wouldn't tell him about his conversation with Milstadt or warn him about what was going on. He wouldn't even say, "Hey, Joe Willie, I'm getting frightened for myself." Or even, "Hey, Joe Willie, I think you should give yourself up." He wouldn't do anything.

Instead when he got home to the thirty-second floor, with the curtains still drawn from the week before, he sat on the floor and smoked. His hands were sweating profusely and there was a pain in the back of his neck. The hours passed and the iguana with the scales along his head and down his back went hungry.

78

COOLEY AND MCBRIDE got the call at four the next day. It was Monday. Be in Taylor's office at six. Taylor and Milstadt had gotten together and the snitch was gonna talk at six. They went downtown together. McBride drove. Kraft had filled them in on everything.

At the D.A.'s office there were reporters. They spotted the two Irishmen on the street and knew the case of Katherine Cleary had moved downtown. Something was up, but Cooley wouldn't talk and neither would McBride. Routine, they said, routine, and flashed their badges to the guard and disappeared upstairs.

Nobody noticed Kraft. He went in another entrance. Or Ernest Fitzgerald. He got there late. And they didn't see Milstadt or Danny. They had gone up early through a side entrance, signed in, got passes, and waited in the room upstairs with the magazines.

The meeting began at six. The room was long and rectangular with couches along either side, a table in the center and Taylor's desk at the top like a crown.

Taylor came down the length of the room. He was in his shirtsleeves and he and Milstadt shook hands for the second time that day. Their first meeting had lasted almost two hours. This time they didn't say anything. Milstadt just turned and introduced Daniel P. Murray.

Taylor stretched out his hand. "I'm pleased to meet you, Mr. Murray," he said. Danny was in a brown suit with a silk tie. He nodded.

Milstadt directed him to a chair at the table and the two sat down. In a minute the others came in and took places at the table. One by one they introduced themselves. There was Lt. Michael Kraft, chief of homicide, Fourth Division, Manhattan; Captain Ernest Fitzgerald, commander, Fourth Division, Manhattan; Detective Tom Cooley; Detective Louie McBride; Detective John Flynt; Detective Steve Clines; Assistant District Attorney William Taylor, chief of homicide, Manhattan; Assistant District Attorney John Briele, prosecutor, homicide, Manhattan.

"Daniel P. Murray," Danny said, his voice almost inaudible.

Cooley was watching him. They all were. He didn't look anything like the sketch.

The door opened.

"Come on in, Steve," Taylor said.

The man was carrying a small stenographic device.

"This is Steve Goodspin," Taylor said. "I think it's a good idea to get this all down."

Then Taylor laid it out for the record. The ground rules were simple. Daniel P. Murray would get full immunity in return for leading the police to a man named Joe Willie Simpson, a.k.a. Charlie Smith, suspected murderer of Katherine Cleary. The authorities agreed to protect the identity of Daniel P. Murray and were never to release his name to the public. In turn he, Daniel Murray, would testify for the prosecution against Joe Willie Simpson when and if the matter came to trial.

The meeting lasted three hours.

Taylor asked Danny Murray his name, occupation, age, and background. Danny answered.

Then Taylor asked another stream of questions and the case of Katherine Cleary came out of the shadows and Danny talked. He answered all the questions and he went back in time to Monday night when he and Joe Willie Simpson went out for dinner. The interrogation went on from there. Danny didn't leave anything out and when he finished, he had fingered Joe Willie Simpson in his brother's apartment in Springfield.

Assistant District Attorney John Briele sat in the pale green room with the hot fluorescent light. "I knew less about the case than anyone," he said later. "I had just finished a trial and Taylor asked me to sit in on the meeting. I knew everybody in the room except the informant. I knew Kraft for years, Cooley, Fitzgerald, McBride, but I didn't know anything about the case and I was listening hard. I had a certain amount of skepticism. You have to. You have to think, 'Why is the guy talking? What's in it for him?' There's always a motive and in this guy's case the motive was perfectly clear. He was involved in a very serious murder. But by the time Taylor finished with him, I was sure he was telling the truth. He knew stuff nobody knew. He knew about Rafe at the bar. That'd never been in the papers. And about the Mickey Mouse drawings, the mutilation of the body, the bathrobe. God, he had to be telling the truth. He had nailed his buddy solid."

Danny was smoking continuously. Sweat was pouring over his face. His thin blond hair was wet on his scalp and his skin was red and flushed. Everybody listened and watched closely. There was no other sound except the movement of the stenographer's keys; and when it was over, the future of Joe Willie Simpson was put in a cage with bars and a lock, and the key was thrown away.

THE MEETING ENDED at nine. Cooley and McBride drove to Kennedy Airport and took the next plane to Springfield. They were going to make the arrest themselves this time. This was too big. During the night nine other detectives from New York flew out to join them.

Meanwhile Kraft and Captain Fitzgerald went to the 20th Precinct and called the Springfield police to alert them and get cooperation. All this was simply a matter of routine.

The two detectives, Flynt and Clines, took Danny home. There, with Milstadt watching, they installed a taping device on the telephone. They checked in briefly with the precinct, where Kraft and Fitzgerald were standing by, and then they all sat down to wait.

The iguana was asleep in the bathtub behind the leopard-spotted shower curtains, and Danny was very nervous, almost on the verge of tears. After a while Clines went out to get him some more cigarettes and Milstadt made some coffee. It was late.

The phone rang. Flynt pressed the button on the taping machine and Danny picked up the receiver. "Hello," he said.

"Hi."

Danny nodded his head at Flynt. It was Joe Willie.

"How's New York?" Joe Willie asked.

"Fine . . . how are you? I've been waiting to hear from you."

"Couldn't do it," Joe Willie said. "I'm all wiped out. Don't know what's the matter with me. All I do is sleep."

"Where are you?"

"Springfield."

"At Fred's?"

"Yes. I gotta get myself together, Danny. This has gone on long enough. I'm thinking of going to Winnemucca. I could make it there."

"Joe Willie, look, I'm pretty tired."

"Okay, well, I'll let you go. I sure miss you, Danny. You take care of yourself, hear?"

"I miss you too, Joe Willie." He put down the receiver and sat with his hands still. Flynt stopped the recorder and picked up the phone and called Kraft.

"Okay," he said, "we've got him. He's at his brother's."
Danny didn't move.

THE APARTMENT WAS empty. It smelled of smoke and
cigarettes and as soon as the cops left, Danny pulled back
the curtains for the first time in exactly a week. He opened
the windows. It was cold and dark outside, and he looked
out over the New Jersey hills.

He turned back into the room. The rug was blue, the
walls gold. The tape recorder was gone, but the coffee
mugs were still there and he picked up the two the cops
had used and went out into the hallway. There he dropped
the white china cups down the incinerator. He heard them
crash and break against the walls of the building, and
then, inside his house, he closed the door and began to
cry.

It was really very simple. He hadn't warned Joe Willie
and he had betrayed him.

He looked out over the Hudson. It was a dark night and
the merry-go-round and the billiard hall seemed like a
long way away.

For the first time in his life, he'd done something he
would always regret.

"Joe Willie always expected people to turn on him," he
said, "and betray him and let him down. I was his best

friend, but in the end I didn't do anything more for him than anyone else. I let him down, too."

Later he would be haunted by guilt and remorse, become withdrawn and lonely. He would wake up in the middle of the night, screaming, sweat pouring off his face, hounded relentlessly by nightmares of Joe Willie. He would see a psychiatrist and relive over and over those few days in January when he changed from a loving friend into a traitor.

One year later, on New Year's Eve, he flew to San Francisco and, almost a year to the hour after the murder, he took a massive overdose of sleeping pills and lay down to die in a park.

He did not die. But from then on he would begin to rise up from the guilt.

BY NINE O'CLOCK THE next morning in Springfield, eighteen policemen were lined up in the corridor outside Fred Simpson's apartment with their guns drawn. Cooley and McBride had been there all night. Others were stationed outside on Delaware Street and at 9:06 Detective Tom Cooley of New York knocked on the door with the tip of his gun.

Fred Simpson opened the door.

The police had no way of knowing if he was the suspect.

Another man was inside lying on the couch, and the instant Cooley saw him, he knew that was Joe Willie Simpson.

The police went in and the man on the couch "looked over at us," Cooley recalled. "He didn't seem surprised. He looked like he felt it was coming. The first thing he said was, 'Let me put my shoes on.' His voice was quiet, easy. He didn't seem like someone who'd done all that to Katherine Cleary, but right away I knew he was."

Cooley, followed by McBride, walked farther into the room. The other policemen stayed by the door, and the two detectives watched as Joe Willie sat up on the couch. He moved real slow and tired. He reached down to get his black boots and pulled them on. Cooley was quiet. So was McBride. They didn't know what to say. By this time Katherine Cleary had become someone they knew and now they knew Joe Willie. They knew a lot, maybe they knew too much.

Cooley told him his constitutional rights, and Joe Willie nodded. Cooley said they were going to the police station, and Joe Willie nodded again. Then he picked up his brown leather jacket and followed the men out into the hall.

At police headquarters a lawyer tried to assist Joe Willie but the young man shook his head and refused to listen. He was taken upstairs to a large white room with fluorescent lights and straight-back chairs. A clerk read him his rights again and Cooley asked him to sit down. He pointed to the chair in the middle of the room.

Joe Willie sat, one foot in front, one foot off to the side, as if he was barely there and might leave. The leather coat was on his arm. His shoulders were hunched and his head bent toward the left. It was Joe Willie's way of sitting when he didn't know if a low blow was coming. He didn't move his head to look at the men surrounding him; he just moved his eyes back and forth, slowly, from Cooley to McBride to the others.

"You want some coffee?" McBride asked.

Joe Willie nodded.

"Milk and sugar?"

"Black."

McBride got coffee. The others got coffee, and nobody said anything. They had no evidence linking this man to the murder and they knew it. They only had the word of Daniel P. Murray, and what case, they wondered, would stand up in court if Joe Willie Simpson didn't talk.

The session lasted almost three hours. Joe Willie was less than an hour from the cornfields as the crow flies, but a lifetime from his future.

McBride thought about the girl from St. Thomas Aquinas Parish, and he began to see what she had found in this man from Illinois. He was attractive. He was tall and broad and strong and his eyes were very blue. McBride could see the two of them standing at the bar, wondering if this was going to be something good for once, thinking it could be, and then, of course, it wasn't.

"We just backtracked," Cooley said later. "We asked him where he'd been. He said he'd come up from Miami. And then we asked him where he'd been before and he said, 'Before when?'"

"Weren't you in New York last week?"

He thought awhile and then he said, "Yes."

"We were playing it by ear," Cooley said, "and he was

feeling us out to find out how much we knew. We got him
back gradually to Monday, and he said he was staying at
a hotel on Times Square. And we said, 'Do you remember
New Year's Day?' and he said, 'Yes,' that he'd been up in
the 72nd Street area, and we asked him what he was doing
and he said he'd met a friend walking, stopped in to have
a drink, and left after a while to go home.

"And I said, 'Well, didn't you meet a guy in the bar?'
And he said, 'You mean the guy who draws pictures?' and
I said, 'Yes; and didn't you meet a girl?'

"He thought, and then he said, Yes, he had met a girl,
and then he left and went home. And we said, 'But didn't
the girl leave at the same time you did?' and he said,
'Yes.'"

" 'Well, didn't you go home with the girl?' 'Yes.'

" 'Well, wasn't this girl Katherine Cleary?' And then,
right off the bat, something was triggered inside him and
he didn't dodge us anymore. The whole thing came pouring out and he told us what happened. And then he took
a pad of paper from one of the guys and he wrote. He
wrote the whole thing out again and signed it, like he was
glad to get it over."

BACK IN NEW YORK, Kraft and Briele were at the 20th
Precinct waiting for a call from Cooley. He telephoned
and said Simpson was making a full confession.

Kraft told him to go ahead and get it all in writing. Then he and Briele went down to court to get an arrest warrant and the extradition papers. They had a quick meeting with Taylor and the district attorney to brief them, and then Kraft and Briele took off for the airport to fly to Springfield.

Four hours later they arrived and went to the downtown police headquarters. Cooley showed them Simpson's statement. It was handwritten, five pages long, in a small narrow police notebook, and signed: Joe Willie Simpson.

In New York that afternoon the district attorney, flanked by the chief of police and the chief of detectives, stood before a crowded press conference to announce that a suspect had been arrested in the murder of Katherine Cleary.

He attributed such success to "good police work," but some variation of the actual truth was already beginning to leak out and the *Daily News* reported: "The girl was killed as the result of a triangle. Her assailant, apparently in a jealous rage, knifed Katherine eighteen times because his roommate had spent New Year's Eve with her."

The next morning Joe Willie appeared in court in Springfield and waived extradition to New York State. He agreed to go voluntarily.

And then, with Cooley, McBride, Kraft and Briele, Joe Willie went to the Springfield Airport and flew back to New York.

On the plane Joe Willie drank a bourbon and ordered steak. When he went to the bathroom, Cooley stood outside the door. Inside Joe Willie took off the gold wedding ring inlaid with diamonds and he bent it crooked against the counter. Then he squeezed it back on his finger and bent it some more until, finally, it was virtually impossible to remove. He didn't want anyone taking it off when he went to jail.

"The plane arrived at LaGuardia Airport at two fifty," Briele remembered, "and was met by a tremendous mob scene of press and photographers. Joe Willie got upset. He said he didn't want his mother to see his picture in the papers and we just told him to calm down and we hustled him out of there pretty quick. Later, at the 20th Precinct where we went to book him, there was another mob scene. I've never seen anything like it. Reporters, photographers, some of them literally could have been arrested for assaulting a police officer, the way they were pushing and shoving to get near this guy."

"Joe Willie hated it," McBride remembered afterward, "and I guess we all felt a bit protective of him by that time. I told him he could put his coat up over his head and hide from the photographers but he held his head way up high. He said he was going to 'take it like a man.' "

The police commissioner was there at the precinct congratulating the commanders and detectives in person. "A fine arrest," he kept saying, "a fine arrest." The *New York Times* asked him how the case was solved and he said, "Through a bit of luck, but mostly hard police work."

Afterward Simpson was taken downtown to the district attorney's office for arraignment, and when that was over John Briele took him to his office. The throngs were finally gone. It was nighttime. "We had to wait quite a while," Briele said. "It took about six hours for his fingerprints to come back and we sat there. We drank coffee and talked —McBride, Cooley, Kraft and me, and of course him.

"He was emotionless, I mean passionless. He was very

calm. He didn't get upset about anything. I never saw him shaking. I never saw him cry. He was a little nervous about going to jail. That was all. He asked me what I did in my work and I told him. I told him too that I'd be the prosecutor on his case. I wanted him to know, but he didn't say anything to that. He looked around the office and asked about this and that and I answered him. Anybody I've interviewed for prosecution, I never have any opinion of them as people. I don't dislike them; I don't like them. I don't get involved with them. I think any prosecutor who does is crazy. I don't think you should ever be vindictive towards a defendant, nor should you ever like a defendant —that is not our job. And if you start getting involved emotionally, then, somewhere along the line, you're going to find yourself in a bad way. As far as I was concerned, my impression of him was that he was pleasant enough. He was very cooperative. He made my job a lot easier because he talked about himself freely. But he reminded me of *L'Étranger* and Camus's existential hero. He was like Meursault. He had no feelings, no remorse. He didn't care. He didn't care about anything."

Cooley was there, too, that night and as the hours went by while they waited on fingerprints and bureaucracy, he listened to the tales of Joe Willie's life that came pouring out—about Miami and the burglaries, about slipping through the windows and taking out the stereos and televisions, about Times Square and his wife, and about not ever knowing which way his life was going to go. He never mentioned the little schoolteacher. It was as if she didn't even exist for him as a memory.

Joe Willie told them a lot about himself and nothing he said was untrue. It must have been a strange time for him, but it was a strange time for the others, too. Cooley, Irish and good and believing, kept remembering Katherine Cleary. No one mentioned her now that Joe Willie Simpson was found. But what about her, he kept wanting to ask Joe Willie. What about her? What do you think about her?

"To be honest," Cooley said later, "the only thing that got me all along . . . we were with him in Illinois, on the plane and on all those car rides, and then up there in the D.A.'s office for six hours . . . and all that time he never said 'I'm sorry.' I know," he said. "I kept waiting to hear it."

Long afterward Louie McBride remembered that night, too. In the beginning he had always assumed the killing of Katherine Cleary was an arbitrary outcropping of madness, but later, he said, he knew it wasn't. "Joe Willie was one of the cleverest guys I ever met," he said, "and everything being equal, you had to be sympathetic to him. You knew he was a born loser, but you had the feeling it wasn't his fault. He was caught up in something that was bigger than he was, and he just didn't have any place to go.

"But the funny thing was," he continued, "she was the same way. She was pretty and smart, she could have been a success. She certainly wanted to be . . . but instead they turned out to be just alike, bumming around in one way or another, trying to get a handle on life, but getting nowhere, I guess, only slipping backward. They were just two people who should never have met."

83

AT NINE THIRTY P.M. Tuesday, January ninth, Joe Willie Simpson was jailed in the Manhattan House of Detention for Men, known as the Tombs.

84

FIVE MONTHS PASSED. Joe Willie was labeled competent to stand trial and the prison psychiatrists diagnosed him as schizophrenic, homicidal, and suicidal. He went to court every few weeks for a perfunctory appearance while his court-appointed attorneys prepared to plead him "not guilty by reason of insanity." His mother telephoned all the time and he told her not to visit. Carole called and he told her the same thing.

And Danny called. Danny told him right away that he had betrayed him and in the telling of it, he started to cry. Joe Willie listened. He was standing up next to the phone on the wall of the jail and he told Danny to stop crying. "It's all right, Danny," he said. "You had to do it. I know you had to do it."

The time passed. He was kept on the tenth floor in the

psychiatric ward because the doctors were worried he would try to commit suicide. But even up there he remained depressed day and night, despairing of the future and the failure he said he'd made of his life.

He told one psychiatrist he didn't understand what had happened with the little schoolteacher. He didn't understand life either, he said, how it worked and all, because, for example, one night—it was New Year's Eve—he saved this woman from a group of thugs. "I actually did," he said, "honest to God. I saved her. And then she didn't even say thank you or treat me right. She just went off."

But then the very next night he said, he meets this person he likes, the little schoolteacher, and now he can't be a man. He's had too much to drink, he can't get it up and he gets yelled at. He gets nothing but pain, for being a man one night, for not being a man the next.

There's just no point, he said. No point at all. And the murder was the worst. Not so much the murder, but now he'd have to be in jail and he couldn't support his wife or make any plans or have any future. It was all over. Nothing, just nothing, had worked the way he wanted.

He got letters in jail, from Carole and his mother, and a man named Stanley Brown. Stanley Brown was a prisoner who shared a cell with him for almost a month before being transferred to a penitentiary upstate and on March twenty-ninth Stanley Brown wrote him a letter.

"Hey, Joe Willie, how're you feeling?" he wrote. "I hope you're feeling fine. I got here today. I was looking for Jerry but I didn't see him. We had hash for chow and I didn't eat it. I hope this letter finds you in the best of health. I have a cell to myself and the bed has a foam cushion for a mattress. I miss you already and I hope you miss me. Take care of yourself and don't worry. Everything will be okay for you. Your friend, Stanley Brown, 166–063."

Joe Willie kept the letter.

The days passed and a man with a crew cut and an aquarium moved into Apartment Seven-One-Five at 253 West 72nd Street. He painted the walls yellow and said he had no idea who used to live there before. Across the street, Tweed's Bar had closed down.

Joe Willie was losing weight and crying often. He saw his lawyer and the social workers and they said he was depressed. He got letters from his mom and almost every day the man down at the end of the hall with the mail handed him a small three-by-five card from Carole Musty. The cards were decorated with bunches of flowers and the printed verse was always in italics, and the words by Carole herself always said things like: "Hi, I love you," "Keep up the good spirit," and "Thinking of you always."

On March ninth, their first wedding anniversary, Carole wrote something longer. "All I can say," she said, "is this year has been one of the most beautiful years of my life."

Joe Willie took all the envelopes, decorated with flowers, and tied them with a rubber band and put them in the white cotton sack where he kept his things.

More weeks passed and on April fourteenth Stanley Brown wrote again. "Dear Joe Willie," he said, "I received your letter and I was very glad to hear from you. We have our phones in our cells and we listen to the radio and television. We get hot toast every morning. I seen Jerry and told him you said hello and I asked him to write you, but he said he didn't want to. Wish you luck. Write soon. Your friend, Stanley Brown, 166–063."

Four days later, on April nineteenth, Joe Willie was taken to Bellevue Hospital. At his attorney's request he was scheduled to undergo a neurological examination to determine if he ever suffered brain damage as a child. If so, it would greatly buttress his lawyer's contention that he was legally insane and therefore innocent. The weeks wore on and he was in a ward with dozens of men in white pajamas. The doctors didn't come and the tests were never administered.

Finally, on May fourth, his bed was needed for another patient and Joe Willie took off his white pajamas, put on jeans and a shirt, and climbed into the green prison bus.

The bus went from jail to jail, leaving off one man here, another man there, and late at night it arrived back at the Tombs, and it let off Joe Willie Simpson.

His hands were in cuffs and his arms were heavy, and there was no one on hand to receive him in the crowded psychiatric ward on the tenth floor where he was supposed to go.

Instead, contrary to orders, he was put in a regular cell on the fourth floor.

He went up in the elevator and along the corridor. He was given a plate of beans and potatoes and put in a cell with one other man who didn't talk. He sat on the bunk and never ate, and listened to the pieces of screams and yells and silence echoing throughout the building. After a while he reached in among the things in the white cotton sack that was his, and found paper and a pen and he wrote a letter and handed it to the guard. "Carole," it said, "this is only to let you know I'm back at the Tombs. I don't know why I'm here, but I am. Love, Joe Willie.''

Then he lay back on his bunk. The place stank of urine and sweat, and reverberated with the high-pitched prison noises of men and metal in constant irritation against each other. In his hand he held his sack, his letters wrapped in rubber bands—letters from Stanley and his mom and his wife—small pieces of hope and a paucity of dreams. And there was no window and no sky, and it was a long way from the fields.

In the morning he got into an argument with a prison guard and threatened to kill himself. "You want me to get you some sheets?" the guard yelled at him as he stalked away. He returned a few moments later with a pile of sheets and threw them into Joe Willie's cell.

Not long afterward, at 12:15 in the afternoon, Joe Willie tossed one of the sheets over a ceiling bar in the cell and, as inmates around him yelled, "Cut up, cut up," trying to alert the guards down the hall, he tied a noose around his neck. Then he stepped off the bed.

The two guards on duty walked toward his cell, and as they slowly neared his cell his not-yet-dead body was swinging, warm, in the air. It gradually died. They cut him down and laid him on the floor.

The City Board of Corrections conducted a special investigation into his suicide in order to determine if it was the result of bureaucratic negligence and indifference. But the question was left unresolved—a matter of dispute between inmates and the guards.

Danny came to the Tombs to officially identify the body, and he removed the gold wedding band from Joe Willie's finger and put it on his own left hand. Then he escorted the body back to Viola Camp by plane. It was laid out at Murphy's Mortuary, only a few blocks from the little white house where he had lived. People came to look at him, six feet tall and blond, once one hundred and sixty-five pounds.

He was buried in the town cemetery at two thirty that afternoon, and at that moment, three thirty eastern daylight time, nine-months pregnant Carole Musty in Miami gave birth to their baby boy.

He was born dead.